ULTIMATE
ÉTAPES

RIDE EUROPE'S GREATEST CYCLING STAGES

ULTIMATE ÉTAPES

PETER COSSINS

Aurum Press

Contents

What are the Ultimate Étapes?

Whether you know them as cyclosportives, sportives or *gran fondos*, mass-participation cycling events have become hugely popular in recent years, largely thanks to the interest generated by the launch of the Étape du Tour de France in 1993 and the immense success that that event has subsequently enjoyed. Nowadays, almost every race on the international calendar features a sportive that presents amateur cyclists with the opportunity to ride on roads that are used by the pros, and I've been among the throng who have relished the challenge and enjoyed participating in them.

Ultimate Étapes stems from a conversation that I had over coffee and waffles dripping with chocolate in a café in Oudenaarde's main square, in the immediate aftermath of the Tour of Flanders sportive. A discussion about the next sportive to tackle quickly progressed, no doubt thanks to that sugar and caffeine rush, to something with a far wider scope in the shape of a Grand Tour of sportives covering western Europe. Thus, the Tour d'Europe was born, which included a broad mix of stages just as races such as the Tour de France, the Giro d'Italia or the Vuelta a España do.

Ultimate Étapes presents 25 'stages' – a handful more than cycling's greatest multi-day races, but we are covering more ground – beginning in York and winding through Europe to finish in Madrid. Taken together, the stages offer as broad a variety of terrain as any of the Grand Tours would provide, from the wind-whipped wilds of the pan-flat coastline of the Netherlands' North Sea coast in stage three, to western Europe's highest stage finish close to the Rettenbach Glacier in the Austrian Alps as featured in stage 12. The inclusion of cobbled routes, the infamous *pavés* that provide the true meaning of 'bone-shaker', and gravel tracks delivers a diversity of road surfaces, as well as exciting routes through Belgium and northeastern France on stages five and six and Brittany and Tuscany on stages eight and 17. The intention is to replicate the different types of challenges that professional racers face when participating in cycling's most exhilarating and exacting events, and to enable riders inspired by the beauty, thrills and demands of these races to challenge themselves on exactly the same terrain.

Looking more closely at the selection of stages, the only criteria I had for choosing them was that each had either featured in a multi-day stage race or is a race in its own right. I've also attempted to ensure that one stage finishes reasonably close to where the next one begins. Admittedly, a couple of large transfers would be required in some instances, most notably to include the stage on the largely unknown Tro Bro Léon route in Brittany. This offers a spectacular mix of roads hugging the region's rugged Atlantic coast, and farm tracks sporting a grassy green Mohican, so seldom are they used. Another transfer is needed for the Baltic to Hamburg route in northern Germany, with its wonderful watery backdrop.

BELOW: Participants in the Eroica sportive roll along a section of white-gravel road on a ridge looking across the fertile Tuscan countryside.

I suspect and hope that my choice will create a debate about the merits and deficiencies of this Tour d'Europe. Before that begins, I'd like to offer a defence of my selection of these Ultimate Étapes. My aim has been to present a mix of renowned and less well-known destinations across as broad a range of countries as possible. Consequently, two of the three Belgian stages are routes from famous one-day races, Liège–Bastogne–Liège and the Tour of Flanders. The latter details what is generally regarded as the classic route that finished with the climbs of the Muur in Geraardsbergen and the Bosberg, and was last used in the 2011 edition of Flanders. Meanwhile, the third stage in Belgium runs through territory that will be much less familiar in the southwest of the country and into northeastern France, mixing rolling hills with sections of *pavé* from Paris to Roubaix. Similarly, the stages in the Alps serve up well-known climbs such as Alpe d'Huez and the Stelvio, but also exceptional ascents that merit arguably greater renown, such as the Grosse Scheidegg and Romandie's Col de la Croix.

No doubt some readers will be disappointed by the lack of time-trial stages, but I felt that omitting them was the wise choice from the perspective of safety. Unlike the pros, amateurs rarely ride on closed roads, so attention necessarily needs to be given to other road users rather than the pursuit of the highest possible speed.

Illustrated with stunning images taken by some of the sport's best photographers, notably Jered Gruber and Tim De Waele, the information on each stage includes a detailed route description, an outline map, a route profile and suggestions on other riding within each region, including details of the most significant sportives in the area. As a result, there are several alternative riding options in the vicinity of each of the 25 stages.

Writing this book over a dismal winter has restoked my enthusiasm for riding my bike. The prospect of savouring every kind of terrain – from coastal roads that at times almost seem to be floating on the waves, to lofty mountain passes that raise you high above eagles circling on thermals – spurs me on as I look ahead to testing my own limits as a cyclist. It has also reminded me what a spectacular sport road cycling is, reaffirming its unique attribute as a sport where the terrain has as much star value as any of the racers doing battle over it. Those battlegrounds are, of course, open to everyone. Any cyclist can test themselves on the same passes in the heights of the Pyrenees where the Tour de France first ventured in 1910, on the cobbles and abrupt ramps of the Tour of Flanders in the heart of bike-crazed Belgium, or on the rolling hills and dales of Yorkshire where hundreds of thousands of fans gave an unprecedented welcome to the Tour de France. Hopefully, *Ultimate Étapes* will provide the inspiration to get out there and try some for yourself.

Understanding the graphics

Where climbs have been categorized by race organizers on the stages we've featured, we have included these classifications on the maps and profiles. These range from 4 for a fourth-category climb, denoting the easiest tests, through 3, 2, 1 and HC for the *hors catégorie* ascents that are above categorization.

All of these 25 routes can be viewed in full detail and downloaded to a GPS device from www.bikemap.net and www.mapmyride.com

To find the routes at bikemap.net simply go to the following URL: www.bikemap.net/en/user/UltimateÉtapes/routes/created/

To find the routes at mapmyride.com go to 'find routes' under the 'discover' tab on the homepage, type in the start town for the appropriate and approximate route distance and the route will be listed. All routes on both sites are entitled 'Ultimate Étapes: ...'.

The Yorkshire Rollercoaster
York–Sheffield, 201km [Great Britain]

If you'd asked almost any European professional racer about England's topography prior to the 2014 Tour de France's Grand Départ in Yorkshire, they would likely have said that it is very much the green and pleasant land described in *Jerusalem* – no mountains, essentially flat roads and lots of rain. The Tour's visit changed this perspective completely, particularly with this epic ride through North, West and South Yorkshire.

The route of the 2014 Tour's two stages through Yorkshire is marked by brown signs that initially point west from the racecourse on the Knavesmire in York towards Harrogate. This opening section is benign, as long as the prevailing westerly wind isn't gusting too briskly. The main road (the A59) arrows towards the posh spa town of Harrogate. Just beyond it, though, the going gets a little tougher as the road climbs up onto open moorland for the first time, heading past the American listening station at Menwith Hill.

Soon after sweeping down past the turn towards Fewston Reservoir and the unforgettably named village of Blubberhouses, the road begins to ascend what was the first of no fewer than nine categorized climbs when the Tour riders tackled this route. Described then as the Côte de Blubberhouses, the hill is known by local riders as Kex Gill, with the eponymous farm at its summit. Make the most of the long, steady descent down into Wharfedale, for once the route begins to climb away from the river with its waters the colour of stewed tea or a strong beer, the climbs keep on coming.

When he was advising Welcome To Yorkshire and the Tour de France organization on this stage, Yorkshire pro Russell Downing said of it, 'There are so many ups and downs to deaden your legs, and most of them are not even categorized.' It is from this point on that this realization begins to grow. The first of many significant climbs that weren't categorized when the Tour passed through is a long drag out of Addingham over Cringles and into Airedale at the small town of Silsden. The next is a widely photographed cobbled hill that climbs up through Haworth, with its renowned parsonage that was home to the Brontë sisters at the crest.

BELOW: Don't adjust your eyes. Yorkshire went Tour crazy when the race visited in 2014 and that included painting the sheep yellow.
OPPOSITE: The Tour peloton riding up the cobbled main street in Haworth towards the Brontë parsonage was one of the most iconic moments of the race's visit to the county.

Beyond Haworth, the route reaches the second of those nine Tour climbs as the road rises up onto the windswept openness of Oxenhope Moor.

The B6113 speeds down into Calderdale and Hebden Bridge. This valley is narrower than Wharfedale and Airedale, the hills looming over the River Calder and the old mill towns along its banks. Inevitably, there's a big climb just ahead, although the rise up from Cragg Vale is steady rather than steep. Surprisingly, this is another 'bonus' climb rather than one of the categorized ascents. At nine kilometres, it's the longest continuous road climb in England. Yet, as it rarely ramps up beyond five per cent, the pros flew up it in the big chainring.

Topping Cragg Vale and riding into Lancashire for a few hundred metres, you're now well past halfway. However, most of the climbing still lies ahead. This begins at Ripponden Bank, which rears up intimidatingly as the road passes the whitewashed façade of the Old Bridge Inn, home to the National Pork Pie Festival at the end of March. The next section is the busiest and most unattractive of what is otherwise a stunning route, taking in the hill at Greetland, bypassing Elland, crossing the neverending flow of traffic on the trans-Pennine M62 and dropping down into Huddersfield.

The Professional Perspective

This is the route according to Russell Downing, Rotherham's former Sky rider who acted as a consultant in the planning of this stage: 'The stage description says there are however many categorized climbs, but there are at least as many again that aren't categorized and therefore aren't mentioned... Once you come off the A59 at Bolton Abbey there are maybe four of them, and riders will start to think, "How many more?"

'The climbing becomes much more serious once you get to Cragg Vale. It's nothing in and of itself, but it's a very exposed place at the top. I've been down to 15km/h going over there in poor weather. Next up is Ripponden Bank, which is typical of climbs in this area. It's less than two kilometres long, but it's really tough, like something from the Tour of Flanders. Holme Moss will be a real test for most amateurs, especially if it's into the wind, but the elements usually play into a rider's favour on the last section into Sheffield. When we go out training we head into the Peaks, as normally we can pick up a tailwind on the way home.

'There are perhaps half a dozen climbs in the Strines, but this route only tackles three of them. But, once again, there are a few others that weren't categorized, although it's good to see that they did use our favourite coming from up Oughtibridge. We all know it as Jawbone, because the jawbone of a whale used to span the road. Often these climbs are tackled from almost a standing start, which makes them even more tricky. And people shouldn't underestimate the steepness and difficulty of the descents.'

This is Brian Robinson's former stomping ground. The first Briton to finish the Tour de France and also the first to win a stage, the Mirfield rider is now well into his eighties, but still gets out on these roads on an electric bike, although he now avoids the area's iconic climb. Rising out of Holmfirth, Holme Moss extends to five kilometres and reaches 521 metres, the highest point on this ride. Averaging seven per cent, it's not overly tough, but the weather and particularly the wind can make it devilishly difficult, especially on its very exposed upper slopes. A word of warning, too, about the descent off it towards the Woodhead Pass. It is steep, has

BELOW: Even seasoned Tour de France riders confessed they had never seen crowds as big as those that packed the roadsides in Yorkshire.

long straights, and consequently, is very fast. Unlike the pros, you won't be tackling it on closed roads, so err towards caution.

The route follows the main Manchester–Sheffield road for a few kilometres before dipping south into the heart of the Dark Peak on the northern edge of the Peak District, Europe's most-visited national park. Comparisons have been made between this stage and the route of the hilly Classic, Liège–Bastogne–Liège, arguably the toughest one-day race on the pro calendar, and this section between Holmfirth and Sheffield is the principal reason why. Known locally as the Strines, the terrain between Midhopestones and Oughtibridge dips and rises consistently and savagely. Once it has been negotiated, though, Sheffield finally comes into view.

The original plan for the Tour's 2014 finish in the steel city was straightforward. The final ten kilometres would be flat. However, Tour route director Thierry Gouvenou took a look around the hills just to the north of the city centre and went exploring. He discovered what has become a legendary piece of cycling real estate in the shape of Jenkin Road, a residential street that rears up so precipitously that there is a handrail on the pavement. For a good distance the gradient reaches an astonishing

BELOW: With the Kex Gill climb at Blubberhouses behind it,
the Tour peloton approaches the hilliest part of this stage.

ABOVE: Although the landscape says Yorkshire, the crowds
packing onto Holme Moss make the climb resemble an Alpine
or a Pyrenean pass.

33 per cent, so ridiculously steep that it's almost laughable. It is, though, the very last time you'll need to engage your smallest gear.

The route finishes adjacent to the English Institute of Sport and its indoor athletics arena. With steelworks close by, the landscape is industrial and functional, and hardly in keeping with the spectacular rollercoaster route negotiated to get there. But fatigue and relief will be so complete that most will be happy to have made it to the end of what was one of the most exciting and best-attended Tour de France stages in recent history.

Sportives

Yorkshire's outstanding event is the **Étape du Dales**, which is organized by the Dave Rayner Fund. This was set up following the tragic death of Bradford pro Dave Rayner in late 1994 and has subsequently funded more than 250 British and Irish riders to chase their dream of a pro contract by racing on the continent. Among those who have benefited are David Millar, Dan Martin and Adam Yates. The book *Everybody's Friend* provides a fascinating insight into Rayner's life and the fund's achievements, which are supported primarily by an annual dinner and this ride. Based in Grassington, just

north of Bolton Abbey, this sportive is held in May and features some of the roads made famous by the 2014 Grand Départ, covering a good part of the Yorkshire Dales National Park. Rated 'very hard' by British Cycling, it offers just one distance of 180 kilometres. **Information:** www.daveraynerfund.co.uk/etapedudales

If that test sounds a touch fiercesome, July's **White Rose Classic**, organized by Ilkley Cycling Club, covers some of the same roads but offers three route options. The shortest is 80 kilometres, moving up to 136 kilometres and, finally, 184 kilometres, going out from Ilkley and around Ingleborough, one of Yorkshire's Three Peaks. The organizers offer women-only start times earlier in the day for each of these routes in order to encourage more female participants. **Information:** www.ilkleycyclingclub.org.uk

There are also two good options on the southerly part of this route. The first is the **Wheelspin Sportive**, which is based in Huddersfield and takes place in mid-April. It offers 40-kilometre, 60-kilometre and 100-kilometre route options. **Information:** www.yorkshireeventsystems.co.uk

Fact File The Yorkshire Rollercoaster

Route Details
COUNTRY: Great Britain
RACE: 2014 Tour de France (stage 2)
ROUTE: York–Sheffield, 201km
TERRAIN: Hilly

Climb Stats

Kex Gill, Blubberhouses
HEIGHT: 301m
ALTITUDE GAINED: 110m
LENGTH: 1.6km
AVERAGE GRADIENT: 6.1%
MAXIMUM GRADIENT: Short sections at 12%

Oxenhope Moor
HEIGHT: 431m
ALTITUDE GAINED: 198m
LENGTH: 3.1km
AVERAGE GRADIENT: 6.4%
MAXIMUM GRADIENT: 8%

Ripponden Bank
HEIGHT: 252m
ALTITUDE GAINED: 112m
LENGTH: 1.3km
AVERAGE GRADIENT: 8.6%
MAXIMUM GRADIENT: 15% near the bottom

Greetland Hill
HEIGHT: 200m
ALTITUDE GAINED: 107m
LENGTH: 1.6km
AVERAGE GRADIENT: 6.7%
MAXIMUM GRADIENT: 9%

Holme Moss
HEIGHT: 521m
ALTITUDE GAINED: 329m
LENGTH: 4.7km
AVERAGE GRADIENT: 7%
MAXIMUM GRADIENT: 12%

Midhopestones
HEIGHT: 341m
ALTITUDE GAINED: 153m
LENGTH: 2.5km
AVERAGE GRADIENT: 6.1%
MAXIMUM GRADIENT: 15% near the top

Bradfield
HEIGHT: 350m
ALTITUDE GAINED: 74m
LENGTH: 1km
AVERAGE GRADIENT: 7.4%
MAXIMUM GRADIENT: 20% initially

Oughtibridge
HEIGHT: 241m
ALTITUDE GAINED: 137m
LENGTH: 1.5km
AVERAGE GRADIENT: 9.1%
MAXIMUM GRADIENT: 15%

Jenkin Road, Sheffield
HEIGHT: 132m
ALTITUDE GAINED: 86m
LENGTH: 800m
AVERAGE GRADIENT: 10.8%
MAXIMUM GRADIENT: 33%

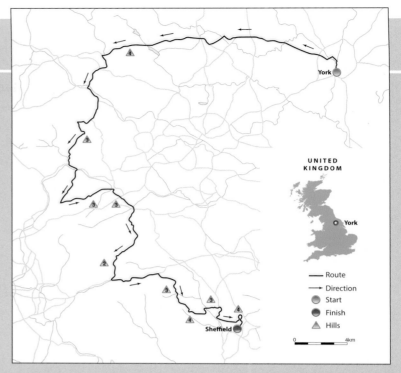

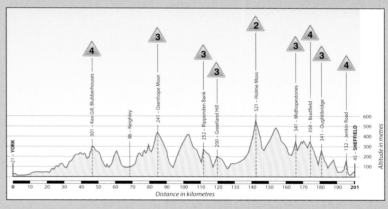

Early July's **Côte de Holme Moss Sportive Weekend** is particularly suited to families. On the Saturday, there is a Massive sportive of 140 kilometres and a Little-Un of 90. On the Sunday, there is a 30-kilometre family sportive. The longest ride includes substantial sections of 2014 Tour stage two. **Information:** www.holmemoss.com

Other Riding

It doesn't take long to realize why Yorkshire has long been the heartland of British road cycling. In the late 19th and early 20th centuries, the bicycle offered workers in the mills and factories of West and South Yorkshire the chance to escape into the hills and greenery that surrounded their smoky cities. The tradition and love for the sport within Yorkshire has continued ever since.

From York, the best options are to head north or east. Either way, you'll soon be on roads that featured in 2015's inaugural Tour de Yorkshire, which is one of the most obvious legacies of the Tour de France's visit. To the north lies the wide-open wildness of the Yorkshire Moors National Park, which is bisected by steep-sided valleys. Among the most celebrated of the climbs in this area are Sutton Bank, which looms to the east of Thirsk, and Rosedale Chimney, a lovely name that belies what is for even the very best a brutal experience. To the east, the Yorkshire Wolds are little known and all the better for that. The countryside is rolling and the traffic almost non-existent. It's an Eden for cyclists.

Further to the west, the big chaingangs from Leeds and Bradford have always headed north into the Dales, where there are as many wonderful cafés as there are great climbs. The big draws are the Tour climbs of Kidstones Pass, Buttertubs and Grinton Moor. To get one up on the pros, take the left fork at Buckden towards Hubberholme and Fleet Moss, the highest pass in the Dales, rather than taking the easier option over Kidstones. Beware the descent into Gayle, though, as it's frighteningly fast.

For star-spotting, take to the roads to the east of Manchester, where British cycling's big names often train on the road when they're not on the track. Snake Pass and the Cat and Fiddle are regular features in Britain's biggest races, and there's plenty of good riding in north Derbyshire heading south from the Dark Park into the White Peak area.

Stage ② South Ups and Downs

Camberley–Brighton, 226.5km [Great Britain]

The longest and, ultimately, most decisive stage of the 2014 edition of the Tour of Britain was the first time that the revamped version of the UK's national tour, which was relaunched in 2004, had ventured into the well-renowned cycling terrain directly south of London. Made famous by the annual London–Brighton bike ride and, in 1994, as the location for the Tour de France's first venture into British territory, this part of eastern Surrey and Sussex offers an outstanding mix of terrain and landscapes. Consequently, its consistent absence from the Tour of Britain's route was a considerable oversight.

However, that changed when some senior members of the professional peloton approached Tour of Britain race director Mick Bennett with a request for a particularly tough stage towards the end of the 2014 race in order to better prepare them for the World Championships a fortnight

later. An ex-pro who had been one of the main driving forces behind *Le Tour en Angleterre* in 1994, Bennett instructed his route-finders to plot out a course that would largely replicate the Worlds road race, where the action starts easily enough and builds towards a lung-busting crescendo. At 225 kilometres, the stage was approximately 50 clicks shorter than the average Worlds course, making it an ideal test of form for that key race.

Considering how heavily populated this part of Britain is, Bennett's team achieved a double success by delivering a demanding route and also managing to avoid the busiest roads. Starting in Camberley, it heads off across the heath and towards Deepcut and then Frimley Green, Mytchett and Ash Vale. Skirting the edge of Aldershot via Wanborough and Puttenham, the route drops down from the Hogs Back ridge between Guildford and Farnham and across the low heathland of Puttenham

BELOW: Alex Dowsett, wearing the Tour of Britain race leader's yellow jersey, tracks two of his Movistar teammates as the 2014 stage into Brighton heads towards its finale on the South Downs.

'We knew when we got to Ditchling Beacon all hell was
going to break loose, which it did.'

Alex Dowsett

Common. After shooting over the River Wey at Elstead, it heads through the sandy heathland of Hankley Common, a training area for the British army that has featured regularly in TV and film, including a number of the James Bond movies and episodes of *Doctor Who*.

Passing Thursley, the road begins to climb seriously for the first time, ascending through Beacon Hill to Hindhead, where it joins the A287. Cresting this ridge, beneath which the incessant flow on the A3 is now hidden in a tunnel, brings the South Downs into full focus for the first time, although there's barely time to consider what might lie ahead before the road hurtles down into Haslemere, where it switches onto the A286 heading due south for the chalkland hills that will eventually provide a big sting in the tail of the ride.

Moving due east on the A272, the route undulates gently as it runs parallel to the South Downs. Passing through Horsham – location of the first sprint on Tour of Britain race day and a good start point for those who don't want to tackle the whole route – Handcross and Haywards Heath, it rejoins the A272 to reach Newick. Little more than 30 kilometres north of Brighton, this village is only slightly beyond the stage's halfway point. Consequently, rather than turning south and heading over the Downs into the regency resort, the route continues eastwards through Heathfield, Horam and Hailsham.

When the road begins to drop down into Eastbourne's splendid seafront, some could be forgiven for thinking that the Downs have been circumvented. Those who do are soon in for a shock, especially if there's a westerly breeze. This would have been providing some assistance for the best part of a hundred kilometres, but turning into it will provide the first of several sapping examinations of strength and endurance.

The first comes straight out of Eastbourne in the shape of Beachy Head. Rising to 160 metres, the ascent to this infamous spot is not particularly difficult. But after 160 kilometres of riding, it will come as a sharp jolt for many – especially if the wind is up, because this road is very open indeed. From the top of this chalkland bluff, the resort of Worthing, which lies beyond Brighton, is clearly visible across the waters of the English Channel. The temptation is to dally, ideally with an ice cream and a sugar-dosed drink while taking in the spectacular panorama – and why not, with another 50-odd kilometres still to cover? Replenish your reserves now in order to be ready for the toughest two climbing tests to come, the category one ascents following this category two.

No sooner have you dropped off Beachy Head than a shorter but steeper climb tugs at your energy levels, before dropping back down to the coast at Seaford and then on to Newhaven, where the route turns right

OPPOSITE: The immense chalk cliffs of Beachy Head loom as the Tour of Britain peloton lines out on the approach to Eastbourne.

Fact File **South Ups and Downs**

Route Details
COUNTRY: Great Britain
RACE: 2014 Tour of Britain (stage 7)
ROUTE: Camberley–Brighton, 226.5km
TERRAIN: Rolling hills

Climb Stats
Beachy Head
HEIGHT: 156m
ALTITUDE GAINED: 148m
LENGTH: 3.4km
AVERAGE GRADIENT: 4.6%
MAXIMUM GRADIENT: 20%

Ditchling Beacon
HEIGHT: 227m
ALTITUDE GAINED: 171m
LENGTH: 2.8km
AVERAGE GRADIENT: 6.2%
MAXIMUM GRADIENT: 11%

Bear Road
HEIGHT: 136m
ALTITUDE GAINED: 110m
LENGTH: 1.5km
AVERAGE GRADIENT: 7.3%
MAXIMUM GRADIENT: 11%

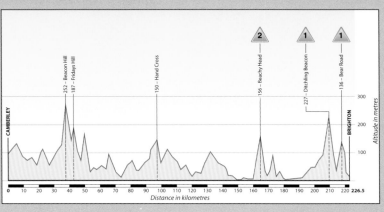

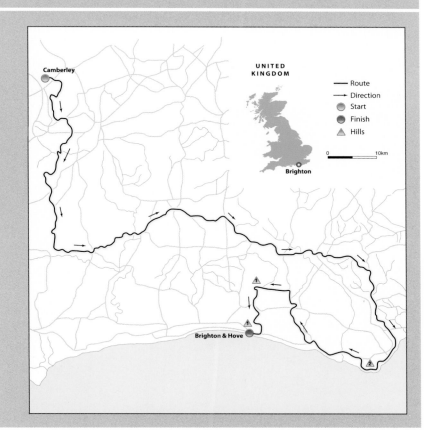

soon after crossing the River Ouse. Continuing on through leafy lanes to Southease and Swanborough, and over the A27 into the pretty town of Lewes, renowned for its unique bonfire-night celebrations, you soon have the rounded bulk of Ditchling Beacon between you and the sea.

Chris Boardman, who finished third on the Tour de France stage into Brighton in 1994, describes Ditchling Beacon as 'no picnic', and so it proved on race day. Alex Dowsett was leading the race when the Tour of Britain came this way. The Essex man acknowledged before that stage that the next few kilometres before the race dropped into Brighton would likely decide whether he maintained his hold on the leader's yellow jersey. Dowsett also revealed that the last time he tackled Ditchling was as an 11-year-old in the London–Brighton charity event, when 30,000 riders head south from the capital and this climb is their principal obstacle. 'We knew when we got to Ditchling Beacon all hell was going to break loose, which it did,' said Dowsett.

Winding through narrow lanes with high hedges that often obscure the climb from view, the route takes a 90-degree turn to the left close to the village of Ditchling onto Beacon Road. The climb starts very soon after. It is a typical South Downs ascent, the steep sides of the hill topped by a much more gently curving and then flat summit, like an upturned cereal bowl. As London–Brighton regulars will be all too aware, the first ramps can be a bottleneck, but those who survive them soon realize that the hardest part is behind them.

Wooded most of the way to the summit, it opens out just before the top, which offers a spectacular view over Brighton and along the coast in both directions. For London–Brighton riders, cresting Ditchling means that their efforts are all but over. Gently at first and steadily more steeply, the road speeds them down to the seafront in Brighton.

Naturally, the pros didn't have it so easy. With the scent of the sea in their nostrils and the prom almost within sight, they switched left onto Bear Road, the final climb of the day. It averages just seven per cent, but there are sections twice as steep and these had plenty of the world's best labouring. Having got so close to it, it's a bit of a kick in the teeth to be climbing away from the finish and re-entering the countryside. But the detour is brief. Before too long, the route bears on to a very rapid descent down to the front. Turning right past the marina and onto Marina Parade, the final flourish is the sweep towards the pier, turning 180 degrees at the pier onto Madeira Drive, where another restorative ice cream is surely in order.

LEFT: Familiar to many British cyclists from its inclusion in the annual London–Brighton charity ride, Ditchling Beacon is not particularly high but was still tough enough to split the bunch towards the end of this frenetic stage of the 2014 Tour of Britain.

Sportives

Although it may not include any of the roads that featured on this Camberley–Brighton stage, August's **RideLondon 100** is highly recommended as both Britain's biggest sportive and one of the few that takes place on closed roads. Following much of the course on which the Olympic road race took place in 2012, the 161-kilometre event starts in the Olympic Park in east London and finishes on The Mall. The terrain in between is not overly taxing, but sharing the road with 26,000 other riders makes for a heartwarming experience. The most renowned section is the climb of Box Hill, although Leith Hill, which precedes it, is tougher. Entry is via a ballot, which closes in early January and attracts up to 100,000 applications. Charities also offer places to fundraising riders. **Information:** www.prudentialridelondon.co.uk

Long a favourite of club cyclists, **The Hell of the Ashdown Forest** began as a reliability ride, an early-season test of a rider and their bike's ability to complete a tough 104-kilometre route. Although still organized by Catford CC, it is now a popular late-February sportive, in which 1,500 riders tackle a tough course that runs from the Kent town of Sevenoaks and over the North Downs to the Ashdown Forest in Sussex and back again. There are seven major climbs, the most notorious of them Kidds Hill in the Ashdown Forest, which has been dubbed 'The Wall'. **Information:** www.hell.gb.com

Organized by Action Medical Research and promoted by their ambassador, TV presenter Davina McCall, **Davina's Big Sussex Ride** is a women-friendly sportive that takes place in mid-June and offers three routes – Cool (34 kilometres), Classic (64 kilometres) and Champion (109 kilometres) – all starting and finishing at the East Sussex National Golf Club in Uckfield. The longest of the three routes weaves through the East Sussex lanes to Battle, crossing the high point of Dallington Hill on the way. **Information:** www.action.org.uk/davinas-big-sussex-bike-ride

As mentioned above, the London–Brighton ride organized by the British Heart Foundation has long featured Ditchling Beacon, but for those who fancy tackling that celebrated hill in something a little more testing than that 87-kilometre run, the **Haywards Heath Howler** is an ideal option. Based on Haywards Heath, it offers the standard three route options, with the epic extending to 166 kilometres and including more than 2,500 metres of climbing. Ditchling may be the high point, but there are several other leg-sapping tests along the way, including the Ashdown Forest. **Information:** www.ukcyclingevents.co.uk/events/wiggle-haywards-heath-howler

Other Riding

The North and South Downs have always been one of the principal playgrounds for riders from London and its surrounds. Given the population density in the southeast, traffic can be an issue, especially close to the capital, but it's not hard to find quiet roads and lanes that offer a nice mix of terrain. One particularly enjoyable option highlighted by the Camberley–Brighton stage is to ride east–west or vice versa in between the North Downs and the South Downs. As the most heavily used routes tend to run from and into London, riding latitudinally helps to avoid the congestion. By piecing together sections from the numerous sportives in this region, riders can come up with any number of options.

BELOW: The relentless rolling of these roads takes a toll, while the wind can be a significant complication because they are so open.
OPPOSITE: What goes up must come down, and these short and sharp hills make for thrilling descents.

Stage ③
Riders in the North Sea Storm
Utrecht–Zeeland, 166km [The Netherlands]

It runs almost completely against logic that a nation where the highest point is just 322 metres above sea level has produced some of the greatest climbers cycling has ever seen, notably 1980 Tour de France winner Joop Zoetemelk, who also finished second in that same race on no fewer than six occasions. That said, the Dutch topography and climate does tend to breed a certain kind of racer, one who is very skilled in dealing with the worst of the elements and is powerfully strong.

Those characteristics are nurtured from a very early age in the Netherlands. Racing on short circuits where the principal difficulty tends to be the wind, Dutch children learn very quickly to line up in the first rank on a start line. When the flag is dropped, the speed is frenetic from the off and it's rarely long before the winning breakaway forms. Miss this break and the wind usually means that there's little chance of seeing the front again. Once learned, this lesson is never forgotten, which is why, despite the odd Zoetemelk, Dutch racers are generally one-day Classics specialists and sprinters, the type of riders who have to know how to race in the wind and how to use it to their advantage.

In putting together this stage between Utrecht and the artificial island of Neeltje Jans in the Dutch coastal province of Zeeland, the organizers of the 2015 Tour de France were hoping that the wind would have an impact on the first road stage of that race, which followed a short time trial in Utrecht on day one. Legendary Dutch rider Hennie Kuiper, another Tour runner-up, pointed out: 'The stage in Zeeland could turn out to be very special if we have some wind and rain. We could even end up seeing some of the favourites losing all their hopes in the overall classification. There could well be crashes, which would split the peloton into several groups, and that's when the tactics really come into play. If you're a favourite and you find yourself in the second group, it's quite easy to lose two, three, four, even five minutes. You never know what could happen.'

As the stage was set to take place in early July and almost exactly five years to the day after a similar coastal stage between Rotterdam and Brussels had been run in very benign conditions, Kuiper's analysis appeared overly optimistic. Even the Tour's route-finders acknowledged that the stage might deliver some rather nondescript sporting fare as race day approached and high pressure sat over northern Europe. The Netherlands baked, temperatures soaring into the mid-thirties. However, as that heat built, the threat of thunderstorms grew. The day after the race-opening time trial, when temperatures were so high even riders from southern Spain were complaining about the heat, barometer-tapping forecasters predicted the weather would break. And how right they were...

'It's always windy and it's pretty hard in these parts. The weather makes riders very tough around here.'

Dutch ex-pro Jo de Roo

Fact File Riders in the North Sea Storm

Route Details

COUNTRY: The Netherlands
RACE: 2015 Tour de France (stage 2)

ROUTE: Utrecht–Zeeland, 166km
TERRAIN: Totally flat
CLIMBS: None

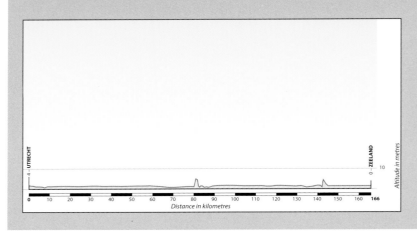

Although the stage began under intense heat, as the Tour peloton circumnavigated Rotterdam the wind got up, black clouds gathered and the temperature plummeted. Within minutes the riders were racing through a blinding squall. The peloton split and split again, leaving just two-dozen riders in the front group and only two of the race favourites: Chris Froome and Alberto Contador. This pair gained a minute and 28 seconds on their principal rivals. When the race finished in Paris three weeks later, Tour-winner Froome's advantage over one of them, Nairo Quintana, was 16 seconds less than that. As Hennie Kuiper predicted, a stage with barely a metre of climbing had made all the difference.

In recreating this route, the temptation for many will be to ride the coastal sections and give the initial inland riding a miss, particularly for those wanting to complete a loop comprising the most challenging sections. However, the route between Utrecht and Rotterdam does have much to recommend it. To begin with, the largely medieval centre of the university city of Utrecht is stunning. Overlooked by the Dom Tower, the tallest belfry in the Netherlands and at 112 metres the tallest building in the city, Utrecht has innumerable architectural delights, while the Oudegracht canal's criss-crossing of the old streets provides a typically Dutch feel. In rush hour especially, it also becomes very evident that the bicycle is the main form of transport, as myriad bike lanes fill with packs of commuters zipping and gliding, bells trilling to warn unwary visitors of their approach.

RIGHT: This remarkable manmade landscape presents a particular challenge, as the elements are sure to have an effect on all but the most benign days.
NEXT PAGE: The Tour de France peloton rolls out through the packed streets of Utrecht at the start of its run to the Dutch coast.

Weaving through the old city and around to the north of Utrecht, the route starts its westward run towards the North Sea as it passes through Montfoort and Oudewater. Passing through the cheese-making centre of Gouda, it turns southwest towards Rotterdam and then continues on towards the coast via Spijkenisse.

Much of the terrain covered to this point would be permanently underwater if it weren't for the extensive sea defences along the Dutch coast. The scale of these defences soon becomes apparent as the route heads out over the first of three dams that are part of immense works that protect much of the Netherlands from flooding. Beyond Goedereede and Ouddorp, the route is right out on the coast. For much of this final stretch, there is nowhere to hide if the elements are in charge.

Heading on to the Brouwersdam, a 6.5-kilometre plug that filled one of the holes in this coastline in the 1960s, it's easy to believe that you're riding across the sea. A glance to either side reveals no sign of land, such is the vast extent of this manmade 'inland' lake. This can be quite disconcerting when the weather is poor and it becomes difficult to discern where the sea ends and the sky begins. The Netherlands is out there somewhere, but where exactly?

Landfall is made in Zeeland at the end of the Brouwersdam. 'It's always windy and it's pretty hard in these parts,' says Jo de Roo, a Dutch star of the 1960s and Zeeland native who is now in his seventies and still goes out island-hopping on his bike two or three times a week. 'The weather makes riders very tough around here', he confirms.

There's barely time to become reacquainted with terra firma before the final stretch on the Oosterscheldekering. Unlike the dams previously crossed, this mammoth feat of construction is a storm surge barrier across the huge Schelde estuary, where tidal flow ensures an almost constant churning of the water. Extending to nine kilometres, at its midpoint on the artificial Neeltje Jans island it has a visitor centre that was the location for that 2015 Tour stage finish. If the weather closes in, it's easy to imagine you're aboard a huge and rather vulnerable ship adrift in the sea, thanks to the roiling sound of the water surging through the barrier gates.

BELOW: This stretch of road along the Dutch coast forms part of the 6,200-kilometre North Sea Cycle Route, which runs from Norway and through northern Europe to finish in the Shetland Islands.

Sportives

Partnered by Maserati, who have been quick to recognize the economic profile of many of the riders attracted to cycling and particularly to sportives in recent years, the **Gerrie Knetemann Classic** is arguably the biggest sportive in the Netherlands after the Amstel Gold Race Tour (see page 34). Starting and finishing in Amsterdam's Olympic Stadium, once the home of Ajax, the city's iconic football team, it takes place in early September and offers five different routes ranging between 25 and 160 kilometres. Celebrating the memory of one of the country's greatest riders, the event's two longest routes reach Utrecht's outskirts before returning north. **Information:** www.gerrieknetemannclassic.nl

For a very different – and multi-day – experience, check out the **Offriding AMS** event that explores the city of Amsterdam via a network of gravel paths and roads. Road bikes can cope with what are fairly fast and smooth gravel and dirt sections on this three-day meander in and around Amsterdam, covering about 350 kilometres over the three days. Offriding is run by former Cervélo CEO Gerard Vroomen, former BMC CEO Andy Kessler and Sven Thiele, whose HotChillee company organizes the pick of the London–Paris events as well as the Alpine Classic

and Cape Rouleur events. In short, the company has a great pedigree. **Information:** ams.offriding.cc/event/ams

Other Riding

Bergen op Zoom is the ideal start point for those who want to include the coastal sections of this route in a circular ride. A very attractive little town with plenty of dining and accommodation options and a long history as a cyclo-cross centre, it has very good road connections. Travel northeast via Steenbergen, Dinteloord and Willemstad, where you can cross to the outer islands and join the Tour route at Stellendam. Once that is completed, continue on from Neeltje Jans towards Kortgene, Goes and Hoogerheide to regain Bergen from the south.

The coastal sections of this Tour de France stage also form part of the 6,200-kilometre North Sea Cycle Route (www.northsea-cycle.com), which runs from western Norway into Sweden, around Denmark and along the northern coast of Germany, continuing into the Netherlands and Belgium before crossing the English Channel to travel right up the eastern side of Great Britain to the northern tip of the Shetland Islands. Much of this epic ride is spectacular, but the Dutch section is especially so thanks to the extent of it that runs along the manmade islands and dams that protect the lowland country from inundation.

Stage ④
Hilly Holland
Maastricht–Valkenburg, 258km
[The Netherlands]

It says everything about the Amstel Gold Race, the biggest event on the Dutch calendar, that its route directions extend to seven A4 pages. What began in 1966 as a fairly straightforward but very long race of 300 kilometres running almost parallel to the Dutch–Belgian border between Breda and Meerssen, which lies just to the north of Maastricht, has become the most convoluted of tests. Nowadays, it is focused entirely on Limburg, the province that dangles like a teardrop off the Netherlands' southern edge, squeezed in between Belgium to the west and south and Germany to the east.

When Amstel celebrated its 50th edition in 2015 and world champion Michal Kwiatkowski claimed the title, the route – chopped back a little to a mere 258 kilometres – comprised four circuits, all of them concluding on the key climb of the Cauberg, the race's long-standing finish that rises from the centre of Valkenburg. The advantage of this format for the amateur rider is the possibility of tackling as many of these loops as physical resources or time allow while always returning to the same point. The difficulty, beyond the hilly course itself, is managing to stick to a course that has as many direction changes as kilometres. With that in mind, pre-programming the route into Strava or a GPS device is very highly recommended.

The man behind Amstel's foundation was Herman Krott, a Dutch team manager who brought through many of the country's biggest names, including Joop Zoetemelk, Gerrie Knetemann, Gert-Jan Theunisse and Leo van Vliet, who is now the race director. 'My dream was to create a true Dutch Classic that could compete with the Tour of Flanders and Milan–San Remo,' Krott expained in an interview not long before his death in 2010. 'I had already figured it out. My race would run from Amsterdam all the way down to Maastricht. Secretly, I had already cycled the route on several occasions, although nobody knew this at the time. Sadly, this route wasn't feasible. Because of all the bridges and detours, the course became too long. That's why we set out from Breda the first time in 1966.'

Krott's dream for the race was achieved within his lifetime. Its roll of honour contains the names of many of the sport's legends, notably Eddy Merckx, Bernard Hinault, Zoetemelk, five-time champion Jan Raas (it was dubbed the Amstel Gold Raas), and three-time winner Philippe Gilbert.

RIGHT: On a perfect spring day, riders taking part in the Amstel Gold Race Tour ease their way up one of many hills on a bike path that forms part of the Netherlands' 32,000-kilometre network.

The Professional Perspective

Three times the champion, Philippe Gilbert explains that there are three keys to success in the Amstel Gold Race: having a favourable wind on the Cauberg so that attacks can be maintained rather than neutered; preserving resources over the long succession of climbs; and getting your position right coming onto the Cauberg for the final time.

'It's a very nervous approach because you are going something like 70 kilometres an hour on the descent, which is not straight so it's very dangerous,' says the Belgian. 'The Cauberg is not hard as a climb in itself – the effort you need is short, but intense. You have to go very deep, physically and mentally, and this takes a lot of energy out of you. It's the kind of effort that I like and am well suited to.'

Gilbert, the only man to have won at the summit of the Cauberg and at Amstel's new finish a couple of kilometres beyond it, prefers the race's old finish. 'I think that it was nicer when it finished on top of the Cauberg because it was more intense and all the fans were there. Before it was like a stadium,' he says.

ABOVE: Philippe Gilbert leads the way on the last ascent of the critical Cauberg climb in 2015.

OPPOSITE: In so many ways this is perfect cycling country, as the climbs are neither too long nor too steep, but by stringing them together riders of any ability can have an enjoyable day out.

Often described as an Ardennes Classic alongside Liège–Bastogne–Liège and Flèche Wallonne, it shares some similarities with the courses of these races and takes place just before them.

Starting in Valkenburg, the race's first and longest loop heads northwards along the River Meuse, or Maas in Dutch, to Geulle and the Slingerberg, the first of a leg-sapping 34 climbs. There are five more on this initial loop, which is the only one of the quartet that lies to the north of the Maastricht–Valkenburg axis.

This loop concludes on the Cauberg, which is not at all taxing taken on its own but becomes increasingly so each time the return comes back to it. Averaging less than five per cent and little more than a kilometre in length, it rises steadily to begin with. The steepest section, which is a shade over ten per cent, lies alongside the town's cemetery as the road traces a long, left-hand sweep up towards the footbridge near the top. Until 2013, Amstel Gold used to finish at the crest of the Cauberg, giving power climbers, *puncheurs* as they are very descriptively known, a significant advantage. However, following the example of the previous year's World Championships that took place in Valkenburg, the finish was moved 1,500 metres further down the road, with the aim of giving more riders a shot at victory.

Continuing through the finish and over the Geulhemmerberg, the course reaches the outskirts of Maastricht where it turns south towards Cadier en Keer. It's all too easy to go off course in this section through Maastricht's very tidy satellite villages. Once through them, though, the

focus returns to climbing. After 20 kilometres without a categorized ascent, the longest break on the whole route, the road undulates ceaselessly as it tracks just to the north of the Belgian border. As the road rolls gently through woodland, the climbs don't amount to much – but the fact that they keep coming so regularly will take a growing toll. In all, they add up to more than 4,000 metres of vertical ascent, which is the equivalent of a tough mountain stage at the Tour de France.

The cumulative effect of that climbing will begin to become more apparent on the approach to the Drielandenpunt (literally the point where three countries meet) at the top of climb 12, the Vaalserberg. Preceding it is the Camerig, which is perhaps the most attractive climb on the Amstel route. It winds upwards in wide switchbacks through thick and often almost soundless forest, although the peace is occasionally destroyed by army vehicles on manoeuvres. To reach the Drielandenpunt, the course switches north to Vijlen and then turns to Vaals and on to the climb, which tops out at 322 metres, the highest and most southeasterly point in the Netherlands.

Heading off the other side of this very notable mount, the road drops very briefly into Germany and then spends half a dozen kilometres in Belgium, crossing the Gemmenich climb on the way, before jagging back north into the Netherlands and retracing the route back through Epen and Schweiberg to Gulpen. After the Gulpenerberg, the terrain opens out, following a shallow valley through rich farmland towards Simpelveld. It almost goes without saying, given the nature of this route, that it doesn't go there directly, diverting instead up narrow and high-hedged lanes through the fields before plummeting back down again. Riding west again from Simpelveld, the route soon returns to the course it took towards Valkenburg 100 kilometres or so earlier.

The third loop commences on many of the same roads as the second. However, rather than pushing into the furthest corner of the Netherlands, it cuts north to Gulpen and one of the most exacting sections of the course. Five tough climbs have to be tackled in rapid succession. The third of them, the Eijserbosweg, with its telltale communications mast at the summit, is generally regarded as Amstel's most testing climb and often has a significant impact on the final outcome as riders toil up the steepest ramp, which is close to 25 per cent. The Fromberg looms moments later, quickly followed by the Keutenberg.

From here the road heads across 'the tops' for a handful of kilometres prior to the fast descent into Valkenburg, which ends with a sharp left turn onto the Cauberg. That leaves the fourth loop. Thankfully, it's the shortest at just 18 kilometres and the easiest in terms of the climbs, although the final four will be far from a breeze after 240 kilometres in the saddle. Even before the fourth and final grind up the Cauberg, many will no doubt have reflected that Limburg may be part of the Netherlands but that it is hardly Dutch in terms of its topography. As the song goes, it's 'Rolling, rolling, rolling … '.

BELOW: The Limburg countryside gets wooded towards the east where it borders on Germany and Belgium.

Sportives

Although the topography of the majority of the Netherlands doesn't hint at it, this is a country with hills. The **Amstel Gold Race Tour** sportive features a good portion of them, especially if you've opted for the full 240-kilometre test that bears comparison with the prestigious Amstel Gold Race that the pros will tackle 24 hours later on many of these same roads. There are no fewer than six route options, all starting and finishing in Valkenburg, just a few kilometres east of Maastricht. The shortest extends to 60 kilometres and the longest to four times that. All feature the same sapping finish up and over the Cauberg, which rises from the centre of Valkenburg and was the finishing location for the 2012 World Championships. Very organized and not expensive compared to many events of similar stature, especially those in the UK, this is a tough test through relentlessly rolling terrain. The route switches back and forth constantly as well, but it is very well signposted and just as well organized. **Information:** www.amstel.nl/evenementen/amstelgoldrace

Although the temptation might be to look south into Belgium for other renowned sportives, look east to Germany and there are some very well-established options, too. Among the best is another event that has emerged out of a long-standing pro race, namely the Rund um Köln. Taking place in mid-June, the **Skoda Velodom Köln** offers two route options of 68 and 125 kilometres. Running into the hills to the east of the city, both feature a lot of climbing through dense forest and stunning countryside. **Information:** www.rundumkoeln-challenge.de

Stretching to 750 kilometres and run over seven days in early June, the **Race Across Germany** is exactly what it says. Starting just over the border from Limburg in Aachen, it features more than 7,500 metres of vertical ascent en route to Görlitz in the east. If that doesn't seem tough enough, why not return a few weeks later in mid-July to tackle its big brother, the 11-day north–south route covering 1,100 kilometres between Flensburg and Garmisch-Partenkirchen. **Information:** www.raceacrossgermany.de

Other Riding

Sir Gary Verity, the man who took the Tour de France to Yorkshire in 2014, regularly cites a long-term plan to make the English county the cycling centre of Europe. However, Yorkshire has an awful lot to do before it can boast a network that's anywhere close to being as comprehensive and well planned as those in the Netherlands and neighbouring Belgium. The Dutch network extends to more than 4,500 kilometres, allowing everything from a short commute to multi-day tours using the LF routes, which range from 20 kilometres in length to 1,300 for the Ronde van Nederland circuit of the whole country. Among those that head into Limburg are the 385-kilometre River Bank Route from Alkmaar to Maastricht (LF7) and the River Maas Route from Arnhem to Maastricht (LF3).

Details on these and other routes, as well as a bike route planner, are available at www.holland-cycling.com, which also provides information on dining and accommodation options.

BELOW: Though less of a factor in the flatter coastal areas of the Netherlands, the wind can have an effect on the higher ridges that are very exposed.

Fact File Hilly Holland

Route Details
COUNTRY: The Netherlands
RACE: 2015 Amstel Gold Race
ROUTE: Maastricht–Valkenburg, 258km
TERRAIN: Rolling with regular short, sharp climbs

The Principal Climbs

Sibbergrubbe
HEIGHT: 153m
ALTITUDE GAINED: 70m
LENGTH: 1.8km
AVERAGE GRADIENT: 3.9%
MAXIMUM GRADIENT: 7%

Cauberg
HEIGHT: 140m
ALTITUDE GAINED: 71m
LENGTH: 1.5km
AVERAGE GRADIENT: 4.7%
MAXIMUM GRADIENT: 11%

Camerig
HEIGHT: 263m
ALTITUDE GAINED: 146m
LENGTH: 3.1km
AVERAGE GRADIENT: 4.7%
MAXIMUM GRADIENT: 8.5%

Vaalserberg (Drielanenpunt)
HEIGHT: 322m
ALTITUDE GAINED: 142m
LENGTH: 3.2km
AVERAGE GRADIENT: 4.4%
MAXIMUM GRADIENT: 10%

Eijserbosweg
HEIGHT: 195m
ALTITUDE GAINED: 81m
LENGTH: 1.1km
AVERAGE GRADIENT: 7.3%
MAXIMUM GRADIENT: 23%

Keutenberg
HEIGHT: 175m
ALTITUDE GAINED: 96m
LENGTH: 1.7km
AVERAGE GRADIENT: 5.6%
MAXIMUM GRADIENT: 17%

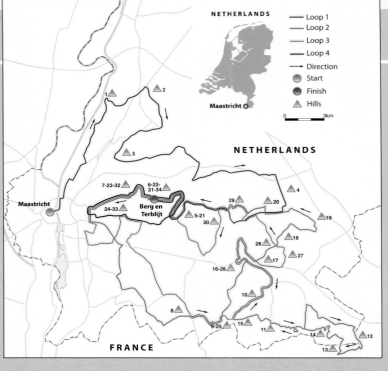

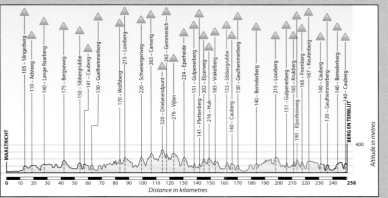

'I think that it was nicer when it finished on top of the Cauberg because it was more intense and all the fans were there. Before it was like a stadium.'

Philippe Gilbert

Stage 5
Hell on Two Wheels
Wanze–Arenberg, 213km [Belgium/France]

BELOW: A wet day on the *pavé*, and this rider is wisely sticking
to the central ridge in order to avoid the pothole-concealing
puddles along the road's edges.

'Paris–Roubaix is the last test of folly that cycle sport puts before its participants.'

Former race director Jacques Goddet

While the Tour de France is undoubtedly in a league of its own in terms of renown and importance within cycling, the question of the race that lies second in the sport's hierarchy can be much debated. The Giro d'Italia and the World Road Race Championship have their supporters, but each lags behind Paris–Roubaix in the popularity stakes, both among fans and professional riders.

To an extent, Roubaix is the polar opposite of its stable mate, the two French events being owned and organized by Amaury Sport Organization (ASO). The Tour stretches to three weeks and is generally decided in the mountains. Paris–Roubaix, meanwhile, is the most illustrious of cycling's one-day Classics, barely includes a rise let alone a hill, and features around two-dozen sections of *pavé*. These cobbled roads might have been the motorways of the 19th century, but they could hardly look less inviting to the modern cyclist, particularly one equipped with a state-of-the-art bike done out almost entirely in weight-reducing carbon-fibre and clad in wafer-thin Lycra. This is a match that is clearly not made in heaven, which supports Paris–Roubaix's billing as 'The Hell of the North'.

In fact, that description stems from the months immediately following the end of the First World War. Prior to hostilities the race had quickly become established as one of the most prestigious on the calendar,

having been set up in 1896 to promote Roubaix, then a flourishing textiles centre very close to the border with Belgium. Looking to re-establish the event following the First World War, race director Henri Desgrange dispatched two trusted associates into northeastern France to assess its viability. Initially, they were surprised to discover how little damage had been done to the roads leading from the French capital towards the battlefields, but as they neared Roubaix that impression quickly altered. It was like a vision of hell, they said, with mud, bomb craters and the charred stumps of trees scarring the landscape. Incredibly, despite the devastation, the race did go ahead in 1919 and Roubaix's status as a fans' favourite has persisted ever since.

This ride gives an indication of the reasons behind Roubaix's standing without committing *pavé* novices to a full-on and perhaps rather frightening commitment to the complete experience. Taken from the 2010 Tour de France, when the race began with a Grand Départ at Rotterdam in the Netherlands and then tracked west via Belgium and on into France, it extends to 210 kilometres between the Belgian town of Wanze in French-speaking Wallonia and Arenberg Porte du Hainaut, which sits at the top end of the most infamous section of cobbles through the Arenberg Forest.

RIGHT: Long reviled by locals and frequently covered over with tarmac, Roubaix's cobbled roads have become a symbol of cultural pride in northeast France.

Fact File **Hell on Two Wheels**

Route Details

COUNTRIES: Belgium, France
RACE: 2010 Tour de France (stage 3)

ROUTE: Wanze–Arenberg, 213km
TERRAIN: Flat, but with several cobbled sections

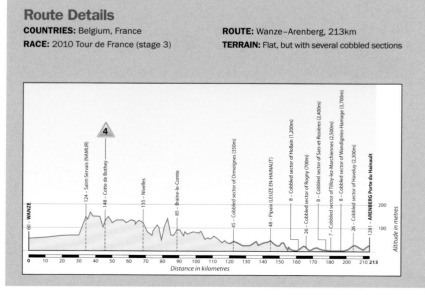

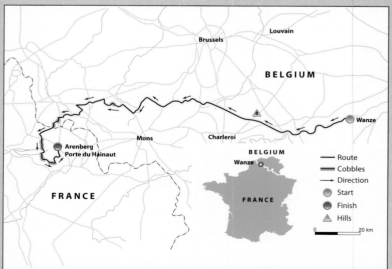

'There's a huge difference between the Tour of Flanders and Paris–Roubaix. They're not even close to the same. In one, the cobbles are used every day by the cars, and kept up. As for the other one – it's completely different... The best I can do would be to describe it like this: they ploughed a dirt road, flew over it with a helicopter, and then just dropped a bunch of rocks out of the helicopter! That's Paris–Roubaix. It's *that* bad – it's *ridiculous*.' Chris Horner

The ride's start in Wanze was a deliberate move by ASO to promote one of the other races in its extensive portfolio, the one-day Classic Flèche Wallonne ('The Walloon Arrow'). That event includes three ascents of the precipitous Mur de Huy in the town just across the River Meuse, as it is known in this French-speaking region, from Wanze. Crossing the Meuse into Huy – where a diversion to the Mur is very much recommended, although it should be pointed out that the 1.3-kilometre climb averages ten per cent and has sections touching double that – the route follows the river upstream to the magnificent citadel town of Namur. This is another regular feature in pro races, although this route bypasses the road up to the imposing fortification and instead takes the road to the northwest and Nivelles via the 1.4-kilometre drag that is the Côte de Bothey.

Rolling gently through mostly open countryside to Braine-le-Comte and Soignies, the only likely difficult for most riders might be the prevailing wind, which comes from a west/northwesterly direction. For, like Paris–Roubaix, this is a route with its sting very much in its tail. A first hint of that sting is delivered beyond Chièvres, where the route enters smaller farm lanes. Between the hamlets of Tongre-Saint-Martin and Ormeignies, a 350-metre section of *pavé* offers a brief introduction to the shuddering experience to come.

According to the pros, the key to success on the cobbles – which for most will be negotiating them as quickly and safely as possible – is to ride on the crown of the road, which tends to be less rutted, and to turn as big a gear as possible. Although it might seem counterintuitive, riding faster ensures that you glide over the cobbles to a degree. This short section, the first of three on the route in Belgium, provides a good opportunity to put that theory to the test. Riding as fast as possible over the cobbles may seem nothing like gliding, as progress is hardly smooth, but it is far preferable to lurching uncomfortably from one bump to the next by tackling them slowly, a strategy that is also more likely to result in crashing.

Once on the main N7 road west, the going is quick again. Bypassing Leuze-en-Hainaut, the route heads towards Tournai, but turns south a few kilometres before reaching this town towards Barry, Baugnies and Wasmes-Audemez. After crossing the A16 autoroute, the route follows the N504 through Maubray and the N503 through Péronnes to reach the second section of *pavé* at Hollain soon after traversing the River Escaut (Scheldt). At 1,200 metres in length, it's much more in the mould of Roubaix's sectors, even more so because the next parcel of *pavé* arrives less than three kilometres later at Rogny. Exiting it, the route skips over the border without a pause.

Only four sections of cobbles remain, but they add up to more than 11 kilometres of bone- and frame-jarring frenzy in the final 28 kilometres of riding. The first starts on the D158B at Sars-et-Rosières. Covering 2.4 kilometres, it merits three stars out of a possible five on Roubaix race day, although it is tackled in the opposite direction in 'The Hell of the North'. Including two right-angled bends that will test cornering and handling skills, particularly if the cobbles are the slightest bit wet, it finishes at Tilloy-lez-Marchiennes.

Barely 500 metres later, the route veers from the D35 towards Brillon onto the D81, the fifth sector of *pavé*. Running 2.5 kilometres to Warlaing, this is another three-star section tackled in the opposite direction to Roubaix. Like the previous sector, the cobbles are generally in good condition, thanks primarily to the renovation work that is regularly undertaken by *Les Amis de Paris–Roubaix*, a group of volunteers who maintain what were until recently unwanted farm tracks but have increasingly become part of this region's sporting and cultural heritage. Beware, though, as there are some sunken sections early on in this sector.

The pattern continues heading southwards. After a brief respite on smooth tarmac, the uneven corrugations of the *pavé* return at Wandignies-Hamage, which at 3.7 kilometres is the longest of the 27 or so sectors that feature in Roubaix. Another three-star segment, its cobbles are well kept. Despite this, those with no experience of the cobbles may find this hard to believe as fatigue and a steady slowing of speed are likely to dissipate the gliding effect required to pass most easily, and also make falling and stalling more likely.

By the final section, this Tour stage is following the route of Paris–Roubaix, tracking through Hornaing and Hélesmes, where the toughest sector running through to Haveluy awaits. With a four-star rating, it is 2.5 kilometres long. Named in honour of five-time Tour winner Bernard Hinault, who once described Paris–Roubaix as 'bullshit', then won it in 1981 and promptly declared, 'I still think it's bullshit', this sector can be extremely muddy. Yet, even if it is dry, by the time most reach the end of it they will be coated in thick dust and look like a throwback to the early days of cycle racing, when competitions took place primarily on packed-earth roads.

Switching north towards Wallers and then on to Arenberg, the route ends adjacent to the mine-shaft lift that remains a witness to this village's past. Now a UNESCO World Heritage site and arts centre, the mine is very close to the start point of what is by far the most notorious section of road in world cycling, the Arenberg Trench, which cuts through a forest where miners once used to relax and forage. Back in 2010, the Tour's organizers decided against sending the stars of the sport into this five-star sector, which begins with a steady drop under a derelict railway bridge, beyond which subsidence has resulted in the most uneven and treacherous *pavé* on the whole Roubaix route. Having come this far, it would be madness not to try it, but folly to give it a go...

Sportives

The **Paris–Roubaix Challenge** is the obvious option for those riders who want to obtain a fuller experience of riding on the *pavé*. As with the pro race, the number and total length of cobbled sections changes from year to year depending on renovation works and other local factors. In 2015, the longest, 163-kilometre option of the Roubaix Challenge's three distances featured 27 sections of cobbles, including all of the best renowned, notably the Arenberg Forest and the Carrefour de l'Arbre. The two shorter options of 70 (with seven sections of *pavé*) and 139 kilometres (with 18) start and finish at the famous velodrome with its concrete track in Roubaix and provide a good taste of the race. However, these out-and-back routes can't compete with the 163-kilometre option for riders who want to immerse themselves fully into 'The Hell of the North'. Bussed from Roubaix in the early hours of the morning to Busigny, they may miss out on the initial 85 kilometres that the professionals cover from Compiègne, but they are spared nothing from that point on. Their goal is to reach the velodrome before it closes at 6pm. Once there, this unique experience can be completed by washing off the day's accumulated dirt in the velodrome's legendary shower block, where the pros used to conduct post-race interviews and each cubicle bears the name of a Roubaix winner. Truly epic! **Information:** www.sport.be/parisroubaix/2016/en

There are plenty of very different sportive options in Wallonia, including those detailed in stage seven in the area where Liège–Bastogne–Liège takes place. As far as this stage goes, riders who prefer hills to cobbles are well advised to consider the **Tour de Namur Cyclo**, which takes place in early May. The three route options (85, 130 and 177 kilometres) all feature plenty of climbing, the longest of the three amassing only a little under 3,000 metres of vertical ascent.

All three start and finish in Jambes and take in the dramatic climb to Namur's citadel. **Information:** www.sport.be/cyclingtour/tourdenamurcyclo/2015/fr

Other Riding

It's rather odd that there is no long-standing sportive that takes in the Mur de Huy, which is one of the most outstanding theatres for cycle sport. Spiralling up the Chemin des Chapelles towards the Notre Dame de la Sarte church that sits in the upper part of Huy on the escarpment running close to the southern bank of the Meuse, it features what is probably the toughest kilometre of road any professional faces during their entire season. Its official average of 9.8 per cent signals it out as special, but at the same time underplays its difficulty, for the final kilometre is more than 12 per cent. For those brave or foolish enough to take its corners on the inside, it's at least two or three per cent steeper again. For the pros, the key to victory at its summit is being able to stay with the best climbers but to hold your acceleration until the line is almost in sight.

This escarpment offers other well-renowned tests, which feature on the 60-kilometre circuit used by both the men and women on Flèche Wallonne race day. Continue on from the top of the Mur and then take the right turn towards Marchin to reach the Côte d'Ereffe. Beyond there at Ohey, the course switches right again. Continue west towards the Côte de Bellaire on one side of Andenne and the Côte de Bohissau on the other. Weaving back towards Huy, the Côte de Cherave has recently been introduced to provide a good shake-up of the field before the riders go onto the Mur again.

South of Huy and Andenne, there are many more climbs of this same ilk. No fewer than 18 featured on the Gran Fondo Eddy Merckx before it was shifted to a new location in Italy. This was based on Andenne and runs south with the Meuse over the Triple Mur de Monty, a big favourite among local riders. Going on to the brewing town of Leffe and then Celles, where it turns back towards the north, it features some of the least known and quietest roads in Belgium, often running through thick forest synonymous with the Belgian Ardennes.

ABOVE: Sylvain Chavanel rides in defence of the leader's yellow jersey over the cobbles at Tilloy-lez-Marchiennes, during the 2010 stage to Arenberg.
PREVIOUS PAGE: The notorious Arenberg Trench, one of the most treacherous sections of *pavé* on the Paris–Roubaix route, which runs for more than two kilometres through dense and damp forest.

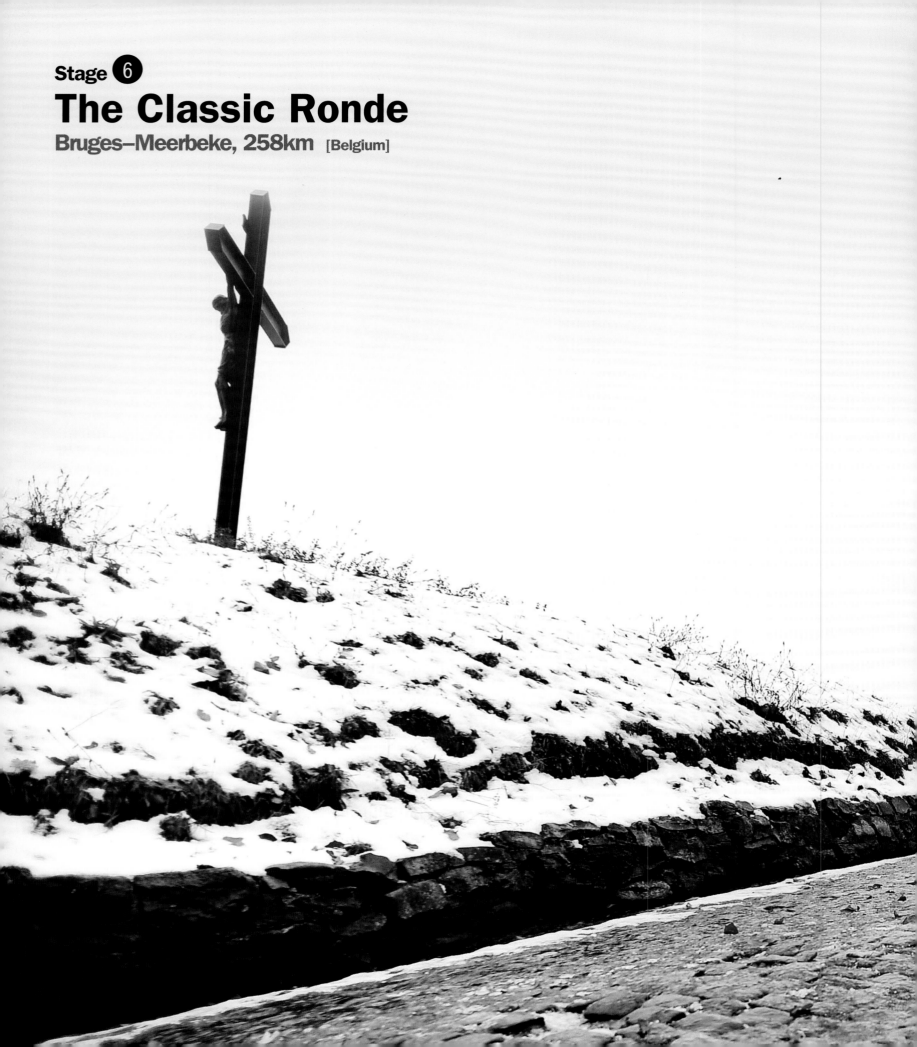

Stage 6
The Classic Ronde
Bruges–Meerbeke, 258km [Belgium]

BELOW: The chapel that sits on top of the Muur de Grammont in Geraardsbergen. Sadly no longer part of the Tour of Flanders route, it remains one of cycling's most iconic locations.

The Professional Perspective

'You have left, you have right, you have down, you have up, you have climbs with cobbles, climbs without cobbles, you have everything. It's a mix of everything. You have to be aware of everything. For me, it's the biggest challenge you can get in a one-day race during the entire season.' Fabian Cancellara

BELOW: Three-time Flanders winner Fabian Cancellara sweeps around a tight turn at the top of a cobbled climb with another three-time winner, Tom Boonen, on his wheel.

No race says more about a region and means more to a people than the Tour of Flanders, or the Ronde Van Vlaanderen as it is known to the Flemish, for whom it has long been one of the sporting and cultural highlights of the year. Established in 1913 by journalists Karel Van Wijnendaele and Leon Van den Haute, the Ronde was intended as a means to assert Flemish language and culture in the face of what was then French-speaking hegemony in Belgium. It is widely credited with playing a significant role in raising the use and appreciation of Flemish.

Stretching to more than 300 kilometres, the original route deliberately ventured into every corner of Flanders. It quickly became hugely popular as cycling served up a long line of local heroes, most of them hulking lads from farming stock who liked nothing more than hammering along in the driving wind and rain on cobbled roads. On the back of the exploits of illustrious Flandriens such as Briek Schotte, Rik Van Steenbergen and Rik Van Looy, the Ronde became one of the sport's five one-day Monuments, alongside Milan–San Remo, Paris–Roubaix, Liège–Bastogne–Liège and the Tour of Lombardy.

In the modern era, the race has had to adapt in order to cope with its popularity. Often overrun by car- and motorbike-driving spectators desperate to see it as many times as possible, it resembled *The Wacky Races*, with unofficial vehicles straying onto the course and official ones often unable to access it. Something had to give and, to the chagrin of many, it was the place-to-place course. In 2012, the organizers introduced a route that featured a number of circuits, enabling fans to see the race several times without moving and, not coincidentally, allowing the organizers to earn substantial sums by selling seats in huge VIP areas along the course.

The introduction of the circuits and a new finish town in Oudenaarde, home to the Tour of Flanders Museum, meant that a good deal of the long-standing course disappeared, most notably the iconic climb of the Muur de Grammont in Geraardsbergen. Disgruntled fans held a mock funeral on the cobbled, topmost section of this mount, the Kapelmuur, carrying a coffin up to the chapel at its summit.

This route follows the course of the 2011 Ronde, the final one to finish in the very unremarkable suburb of Meerbeke in the town of Ninove. It begins in the much more inspiring setting of the Grote Markt in the centre of Bruges. Rather than heading out to the windswept North Sea coast, as it would traditionally have done when the length of the course still approached 300 kilometres, this edition of the Ronde had other ways to sap the juice from racers' legs. There were no fewer than 16 climbs packed into the second half of the race, ten of them cobbled.

After arrowing due south through Hille and Ingelmunster, then entering Kortrijk from the west via Izegem and Gullegem, the route heads eastward towards Meerbeke. Leaving Kortrijk – an ideal alternative start point for those who want to keep the distance down a little – the course begins to meander as it closes on the first climb, the Tiegemberg, one of the few where the cobbles have disappeared under tarmac. The first cobbled ascent comes soon after in the shape of the Nokereberg. It's small fry, though, compared with what's to come.

Continuing into Wanngem and Lede, there's a Roubaix-like surprise awaiting in the shape of a two-kilometre section of cobbles. Bottles can be shaken loose, spares sent flying. The secret, as on Roubaix's *pavé*, is to maintain as high a speed as possible and not grip the bars too tightly. Stay relaxed.

BELOW: Flanders' cobbled hills are renowned, but its route also features several long, flat sections over the *kassei*, as they are known by the locals.

PREVIOUS PAGE: Busy in the spring when the cycling world's focus is on it, the Flemish Ardennes can be beautifully quiet at the other end of the season.

Crossing the Scheldt at Oudenaarde, the route passes the Centrum Ronde Van Vlaanderen, where legendary Flemish sprinter Freddy Maertens works as a consultant, and heads out into the farmland below the ridge of the Flemish Ardennes. Here the ride's main difficulties are hidden among the trees and hedgerows.

The signal of a change in emphasis arrives at Roborst, where a flat, 300-metre cobbled section provides another test of whether riders have got everything secured properly. Given the fuss and focus about the Ronde's bergs, it's all too easy to overlook its cobbled pavements, of which there are half a dozen. The longest of them is Paddestraat, which is more than two kilometres long and starts with a quick descent into a sharpish right-hander that tends to elicit a beam of delight tinged with fear. In the wet, this short section is among the most perilous on the route.

You're barely off it when the 1.3-kilometre run along Lippenhovestraat's cobbles begins.

Scooting over the Rekelberg and Kaperij, which are both well surfaced, the route begins to twist and turn every few hundred metres, as if tracing the meanderings of a fly across the race map. Every few kilometres, a tight turn leads onto a climb. The Kruisberg and Knokteberg follow in quick succession, the first a combination of tarmac and cobbles, the second the steepest ascent so far. Like all of the Ronde's climbs, these are more suited to power riders than pure climbers, to those who can churn a big gear while still in the saddle and in spite of the jarring effect of the cobbles.

It's brute force that really counts, and particularly on climbs like the Oude Kwaremont, which is next up. It averages four per cent, but read nothing into that. Cobbled for two and a half kilometres, it starts gently, barely rising as it passes between small fields and enclosures. But it steadily steepens, then gets more abrupt and yet more again the further it goes on. Ignore the temptation to stand on the pedals, especially if it's wet, because your wheels will lose traction and start to spin. The trick is to keep pushing as big a gear of possible with all you've got in your thighs and lower back. Feel that muscle burn and relish it. This is what the Ronde is all about. It's like arm-wrestling on a bike. The strongest always prevail.

After one Ronde icon come two more. Only 360 metres long, the Paterberg is the steepest climb all day, averaging 12 per cent and touching 20 on occasions. It's made more difficult, as it begins with what is almost a dead turn, which means you can carry little speed onto it. For bigger riders, it offers a chance to turn the tables on the spring-heeled mountain goats in your group. This is your opportunity to drop them on a climb, or at the very least roughen them a little for the infamous hill only a few corners away.

Introduced into the Tour of Flanders in 1976 – Eddy Merkcx complained that riders might as well bring a ladder to scale it – the Koppenberg's infamous reputation stems from an incident in 1987. Leading the race onto the climb, tiring Danish rider Jesper Skibby lost his balance on the steepest section and fell onto the cobbles, leaving the driver of the official race car just behind him with a difficult decision: either stop and hold up the peloton fast closing in, or press on. He took the latter option, driving over the prone Skibby's bike and narrowly missing his legs. Dropped from the route after that season because it was deemed too dangerous, the climb was reintroduced in 2002 and has featured in most years since.

Although its average gradient is a little lower than the Paterberg, the Koppenberg is almost twice as long, is steeper in parts and narrower, too. These three factors tend to result in mayhem when large groups reach its wicked slope, as someone is sure to run out of momentum and come to an abrupt halt, causing a domino effect behind them. On days when there are fewer cyclists about, it's a hard grind, but most riders should be able to conquer it given a clear run at its initial ramp.

The modern version of Flanders tackles this trio of climbs three times each, which may make for a more gripping spectacle, but is surely too much of a good thing if you're riding them. This is where the old route wins out, offering more variety, which means more of the area's legendary climbs. They appear quickly too, Steenbeekdries, the Taaienberg and the

Eikenberg following in rapid succession. There is a bit of respite before the Molenberg, and then a bit more as the next three climbs are on asphalt rather than cobbles.

Coming off the last of these three, the Tenbosse, the route is running east again towards Ninove and the final two difficulties. The first arrives almost immediately after crossing the river in Geraardsbergen. The Muur de Grammont (higher up it becomes the Kapelmuur) rises for more than a kilometre from the town's centre. Thanks to regular traffic and repair, its cobbles are smooth and even, but there's no escaping the ever-increasing gradient. Switching right onto the narrower Kapelmuur, it rears up. As the chapel starts to loom up above, it veers right again, steeper than before. This was one of the most critical points in the Ronde, so often the place where it was won and lost.

ABOVE: The Koppenberg, a climb where the very best can end up walking after even the slightest loss of momentum. Cycling's greatest racer, Eddy Merckx, once suggested that riders might as well carry ladders in order to scale it.

Just one more cobbled test remains. Lined by terraced houses, the Bosberg is not as impressive as the Muur, nor as steep. But it was another key strategic point, the cobbled section towards the top offering riders who weren't sprinters the final chance to drop any speedsters. Cresting it, just 12 kilometres remain before the right turn onto Halsesteenweg in Meerbeke and the long drag up to the finish, next to the school on the left. It's rather mundane and hardly in keeping with what has gone before. Yet on the day of the Ronde, this was the centre of Flanders, the focus for half of the Flemish population either watching at the roadside or on TV, willing one of their own to victory.

Sportives

The **Ronde Van Vlaanderen Cyclo** is one of the biggest and best-organized sportives. It takes place the day before the pros take on their own Flanders challenge and offers 16,000 riders the choice of three courses, covering 71, 127 and 239 kilometres respectively. Of the three, the middle distance is the most preferred option because it features all of the celebrated climbs but is only half as long as the full-on Ronde experience. Riders tackling the latter start in the early morning darkness in Bruges (lights are compulsory) and cover more than 100 kilometres of

Fact File The Classic Ronde

Route Details

COUNTRY: Belgium
RACE: Tour of Flanders (2011)
ROUTE: Bruges–Meerbeke, 258km
TERRAIN: Flat initially, then numerous short, steep climbs

The Principal Climbs

Kruisberg
HEIGHT: 119m
ALTITUDE GAINED: 87m
LENGTH: 1.8km
AVERAGE GRADIENT: 4.8%
MAXIMUM GRADIENT: 9%

Oude Kwaremont
HEIGHT: 111m
ALTITUDE GAINED: 93m
LENGTH: 2.2km
AVERAGE GRADIENT: 4.2%
MAXIMUM GRADIENT: 11.6%

Paterberg
HEIGHT: 80m
ALTITUDE GAINED: 48m
LENGTH: 0.36km
AVERAGE GRADIENT: 12.9%
MAXIMUM GRADIENT: 20.3%

Koppenberg
HEIGHT: 77m
ALTITUDE GAINED: 64m
LENGTH: 0.6km
AVERAGE GRADIENT: 11.6%
MAXIMUM GRADIENT: 22%

Eikenberg
HEIGHT: 87m
ALTITUDE GAINED: 65m
LENGTH: 1.2km
AVERAGE GRADIENT: 6.2%
MAXIMUM GRADIENT: 10%

Muur de Grammont
HEIGHT: 101m
ALTITUDE GAINED: 68m
LENGTH: 1km
AVERAGE GRADIENT: 6.8%
MAXIMUM GRADIENT: 19.8%

Bosberg
HEIGHT: 105m
ALTITUDE GAINED: 67m
LENGTH: 1.35km
AVERAGE GRADIENT: 5%
MAXIMUM GRADIENT: 11%

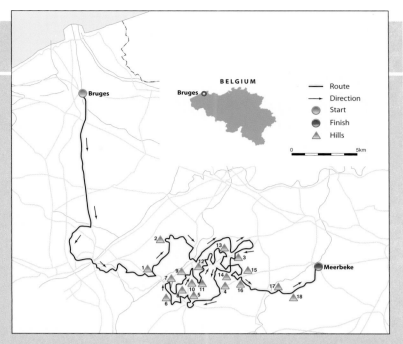

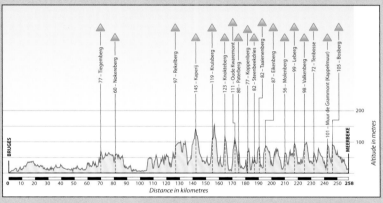

mainly flat roads, reaching the hills at the same point as those who opted for the middle route. The only drawback of the RVV Cyclo are the huge numbers on the road, which can make negotiating the climbs very difficult, particularly on the Koppenberg where only the very early and late starters usually have the chance of an unhindered run. Almost everyone else walks up this fabled climb. **Information:** www.rondevanvlaanderen. be/en

Starting and finishing in Aalst, the **Peter Van Petegem Classic** pays tribute to the Flemish two-time winner of the Ronde with an event offering four route options that are between 80 and 160 kilometres in length. The longest option includes 11 climbs in the Flemish Ardennes, notably the Muur, Bosberg and Molenberg. Taking place a couple of weeks after the RVV Cyclo, it is a much more low-key sportive and all the better for that. **Information:** www.sport.be/cyclingtour/petervanpetegemclassic

For a very different perspective on Flanders, August's **Decathlon Classic** is well worth a look. Based on the university town of Leuven, to the east of Brussels, it offers of 91, 134 and 169 kilometres, the latter featuring no fewer than 18 climbs. **Information:** www.sport.be/cyclingtour/2016/fr/kalender

Other Riding

Using Kortrijk, Oudenaarde or Geraardsbergen as a base, there are numerous options in all directions, all well signposted and often using designated cycle paths. West of Kortrijk is the Kemmelberg, the main climb in the Ghent–Wevelgem race, a cobbled beauty with a devilish descent off the other side. Oudenaarde and Geraardsbergen are in the heart of Tour of Flanders country and there is no shortage of other climbs in these areas that have featured in the Ronde at one time or another. Of the 57 that have appeared since the first running in 1913, Berendries (in Sint-Maria-Oudenhove), the Edelareberg (Edelare), Hotond–Hoogberg (Zulzeke), the Valkenberg (Nederbrakel), Varentberg (Mater), Volkegemberg (Volkegem) and the Wolvenberg (Volkegem) appeared regularly before the route's overhaul in 2012.

The Toughest Day on the Calendar
Liège–Bastogne–Liège, 253km [Belgium]

In terms of the physical test it sets, Liège–Bastogne–Liège is widely believed to be the toughest one-day race on the professional calendar. Although dwarfed in distance by Milan–San Remo and by no means as brutally savage as Paris–Roubaix, the stand-out race in French-speaking Wallonia serves up around 4,700 metres of climbing, putting it on a par with the toughest mountain stages ever seen in the three-week Grand Tours.

Its status as the oldest race on the calendar has earned it the nickname '*La Doyenne*'. Founded in 1892 by enthusiasts who had plans to organize a Liège–Paris–Liège event – having witnessed the popular success of the 1,100-kilometre Paris–Brest–Paris race that took

place for the first time the previous year – it has become one of the five Monuments. It has a particular edge because it is one of the few one-day races that tempts the Grand Tour specialists into a one-off contest.

Why Liège–Bastogne–Liège? When the first editions took place, the race officials were dependent on the train to get about and it took them south from Liège to Bastogne, deep in the Ardennes Forest and close to the border with Luxembourg. The officials would travel south, see the racers through the checkpoint at Bastogne, then chug north again to be ready for them at the finish.

Like any good Classic, most of Liège's principal tests are packed

'It is the most beautiful race in the world, at least it is to me. I would certainly have swapped the races I'd won to win Liège–Bastogne–Liège.'

Philippe Gilbert

into its final quarter. However, the characteristic ripples and rolls of the Ardennes are guaranteed to deplete a rider's reserves almost from the start in the centre of Liège. The weather is often a factor, too, in this region, even in what are supposed to be some of the most clement of months. It should be remembered that arguably the most renowned Classic in history took place here in 1980, when Bernard Hinault rode through blizzard conditions to win *La Doyenne*, finishing nine minutes ahead of the runner-up. He was one of only 21 men to complete the course on a day when more than 150 riders abandoned, some as early as on the first climb out of Wallonia's principal city.

BELOW: The early morning sun warms a small group of riders climbing through open farmland in the Belgian Ardennes.

The outward leg of the course crosses the inward at Remouchamps, where a huge viaduct carries the A26 north–south autoroute over the town. The buzz of traffic soon disappears, though, as the course continues on through Aywaille and then south into the Belgian province of Luxembourg. Approaching La Roche-en-Ardenne, the road cuts through the thick forest that provides a reminder of this region's principal reason for notoriety, the German counter-offensive of late 1944 that became known as the Battle of the Bulge. By attacking with tank divisions through the Ardennes Forest, which the Allies believed was too impenetrable for any kind of offensive, the German forces quickly pushed a long way into enemy territory, creating the bulge. The attack was stymied when the Germans' supply lines became overly stretched, leaving their tanks short of fuel and enabling the Allies to push them back.

The battle is remembered in several places along this route, initially in La Roche-en-Ardenne, where an American Sherman and a British M-10 Achilles tank commemorate the liberation of the town in January 1945. On the road out of La Roche and its dramatic castle, the route heads up *La Doyenne*'s first categorized climb. Between Bertogne and Bastogne, it rises further still onto a plateau. By the time the road reaches the garrison town of Bastogne, where there are more reminders of the Second World War tank battle, the road is well above 500 metres and very open to the elements.

Bastogne is a good place to refuel and stock up on supplies. The road back north to Liège is half as long again as the run south, and far lumpier. It starts in undemanding fashion, aiming straight across the tops towards

The Professional Perspective

'It's the most beautiful of the Classics. Like the Tour of Lombardy, if you're riding well you're going to be at the front. You're not sure of winning, but in races like that, when you are strong it is much easier. Compared to the Tour of Flanders or Milan–San Remo, there are also a lot fewer risks. In those races, when you're 80 kilometres from the finish, you look around and see there are still lots of big names. At Liège, when riders are dropped, they can't work their way back up to the front.' Sean Kelly

BELOW: Completely enchanting on a benign day, these forest roads take on a tougher complexion when the weather turns.
OPPOSITE: Renowned for its dense forest, the Ardennes can feel like a forgotten world thanks to roads that are extremely quiet.

Houffalize, a regular rendezvous for the world's leading mountain bikers. There is a sharp drop into the town, and this is mirrored by the climb away from it. The Côte de Saint-Roch is one of the most photographed locations in professional cycling. On Liège race day, the peloton has to squeeze through the packed ranks of flag-waving fans, and the result is a river of humanity rising between the houses on each side.

Continuing north on main roads, which aren't too busy as the autoroute is not very far away, the route soon passes through Vielsalm and enters the province of Liège, which marks a change of atmosphere. Nearing Neuville, there is a switch to the right onto a lane that rises for more than two kilometres to the summit of the Côte de Wanne. Passing the memorial to the men of the US 517th Parachute Regimental Combat Team and ignoring the left turn towards the 'Piste de Ski, Van de Wanne', which underlines how fierce the elements can get here at an altitude of just 500 metres, the route soon shoots down into the edge of Stavelot.

As it arrives at another set of Second World War vehicles commemorating liberation from Nazi occupation, the route turns savagely backwards and upwards onto the Côte de Stockeu, once one of Eddy Merckx's favourite stomping grounds. It's only a kilometre long but averages more than 12 per cent, which feels a lot steeper when you can carry almost no momentum onto it. It's a hard grind until you find the correct gear and are able to get your climbing legs spinning. But it's not long before the memorial to Merckx at its summit comes into view, signalling another 180-degree turn and a very fast plunge back into Stavelot, crossing the river, bouncing through its cobbled centre, out the other side and straight onto the Côte de la Haute Levée.

Quite abrupt initially, the Haute Levée eases a touch and becomes a long drag through woodland, from which the roar of testing at the Spa-Francorchamps motor-racing circuit can often be heard. It was on this climb that Bernard Hinault made his winning move in 1980, although it was hardly planned. Leading the front group, the Frenchman set the pace for some time, climbing away from Stavelot and eventually flicking his elbow to encourage the rider behind to come through. No one did. He flicked again. Still no one. Hinault looked around. He was on his own. He remained so all the way into the finish, by which point he was so cold he couldn't raise his arms to celebrate victory. Decades later, the Frenchman still loses the feeling in three of his fingers when the temperature falls into single figures.

After topping the Haute Levée, the route soon turns onto small lanes, weaving through woods and between fields to reach the Col du Rosier, the most attractive climb all day, cutting through the trees with barely any traffic to disturb the peace. At 565 metres, this is the high point of the ride. From it, there's a fast descent into Spa, where the route turns west over the Col du Maquisard and drops down into Remouchamps, crossing the route of the outward leg and following the riverbank briefly before weaving through back streets to the foot of La Redoute.

In contrast to the calm of the Rosier, this climb hums with constant noise from the A26 autoroute that runs parallel to it. Yet the shock of the steep opening ramps and the names painted on the road make it easy to block out the racket of vehicles hurtling down towards Remouchamps and straining up the carriageway from it. One name stands out – PHIL. Repeated over and over, it refers to local star Philippe Gilbert, who won Liège in 2011. The climb soon elbows away from the autoroute and returns to the quiet of the lanes heading through Sprimont, Dolembreux and Méry. After a tight turn over a railway crossing, the penultimate climb begins.

BELOW: The hills in the Ardennes are not especially high, but they climb to plateaux that are very exposed and susceptible to rapid changes in the weather.

Route Details

COUNTRY: Belgium
RACE: Liège–Bastogne–Liège
ROUTE: Liège–Bastogne–Liège, 253km
TERRAIN: Rolling, with regular 2–4km climbs

The Principal Climbs

Côte de Saint-Roch
HEIGHT: 457m
ALTITUDE GAINED: 127m
LENGTH: 1.15km
AVERAGE GRADIENT: 11%
MAXIMUM GRADIENT: 15%

Côte de Wanne
HEIGHT: 495m
ALTITUDE GAINED: 167m
LENGTH: 2.2km
AVERAGE GRADIENT: 7.6%
MAXIMUM GRADIENT: 12%

Côte de Stockeu
HEIGHT: 400m
ALTITUDE GAINED: 120m
LENGTH: 1km
AVERAGE GRADIENT: 12%
MAXIMUM GRADIENT: 15%

Côte de la Haute Levée
HEIGHT: 506m
ALTITUDE GAINED: 203m
LENGTH: 3.6km
AVERAGE GRADIENT: 5.6%
MAXIMUM GRADIENT: 13%

Col du Rosier
HEIGHT: 565m
ALTITUDE GAINED: 255m
LENGTH: 4.5km
AVERAGE GRADIENT: 5.7%
MAXIMUM GRADIENT: 9%

Côte de la Redoute
HEIGHT: 292m
ALTITUDE GAINED: 161m
LENGTH: 1.7km
AVERAGE GRADIENT: 9.5%
MAXIMUM GRADIENT: 17%

Côte de la Roche aux Faucons
HEIGHT: 269m
ALTITUDE GAINED: 188m
LENGTH: 4.6km
AVERAGE GRADIENT: 4%
MAXIMUM GRADIENT: 11%

Côte de Saint-Nicolas
HEIGHT: 172m
ALTITUDE GAINED: 100m
LENGTH: 1.2km
AVERAGE GRADIENT: 8.6%
MAXIMUM GRADIENT: 11%

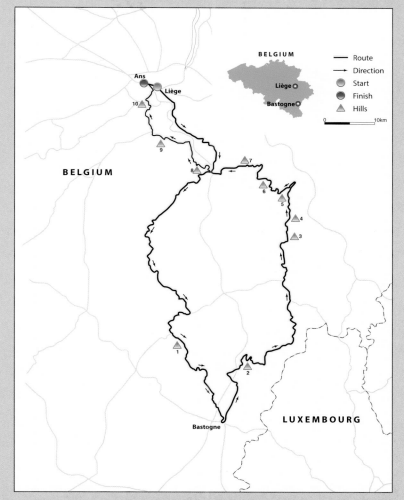

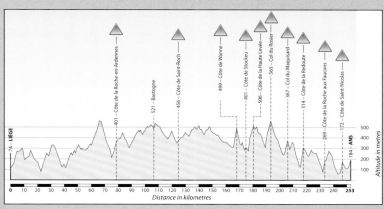

Rising precipitously through a plush neighbourhood, the Côte de la Roche aux Faucons gets its name from the 'falcons' rock' look-out high above a huge swirl of a bend in the River Ourthe. The climb eases slightly as it reaches the path to the look-out, then rears up again through the meadows and eventually emerges onto a busy highway into Liège. Passing over this, the route descends quickly into the industrial centre of Seraing and springs over the Meuse, to the rust-coloured Standard Liège football ground.

La Doyenne used to follow the Meuse into the centre of Liège, but for the last few years it has finished in the suburb of Ans. So, the route jags back behind the stadium and tracks through more industrial wasteland, continuing into the working-class area of Saint-Nicolas, where many Italians settled in the post-war years having come north looking for work. The climb through it is hardly scenic, but it's tough enough that you'll barely notice.

A handful of kilometres further on, the final kilometre begins. Naturally, this being the hilliest race of the season, it's uphill, initially on the Rue Walthère Jamar, then turning left onto the Rue Jean Jaurès, where it concludes in rather mundane fashion outside a Carrefour supermarket and Pizza Hut. The setting is hardly in keeping with the grandness of the scenery and the challenge that has gone before. Mind you, after 4,500 metres and more of climbing, most won't complain about the opportunity for a restorative slice or two.

Sportives

Organized by the Golazo group behind the Ronde Van Vlaanderen Cyclo, the **Liège–Bastogne–Liège Challenge** takes place the day before the pro race in late April. Its route varies slightly as it starts and finishes in Liège, resulting in the longest route extending to 273 kilometres, 20 more than the professionals cover, making it one of the toughest sportives on the calendar. There are two shorter options: the 156-kilometre route goes out to Stavelot and back, including all the climbs from the Haute Levée onwards; and the 75-kilometre route goes out to Remouchamps and back, tackling La Redoute, La Roche aux Faucons and Saint-Nicolas. **Information:** www.sport.be/lblcyclo/2016/en

Run a month after the Liège Challenge, **Tilff–Bastogne–Tilff** covers some of the same ground, but has a slightly different aspect, particularly towards the finish. Starting and finishing in Angleur, south of Liège, it has three route options (88, 157 and 254 kilometres) and just as much climbing, although many of the hills are different; the Côte de Wanne, Col du Rosier and La Redoute do feature, though. It attracts more than 5,000 riders. **Information:** www.sport.be/cyclingtour/tilffbastognetilff/2016/fr

Based on Spa, early May's **Flèche du Wallonie** offers four route options (89, 136, 176 and 217 kilometres) and covers the terrain midway between Liège and Bastogne, including the most celebrated climbs. The longest option roams far enough west to include roads that have often featured in the Flèche Wallonne in the days when it was almost 300 kilometres long, thereby providing an insight into both Ardennes Classics on the same day. **Information:** www.cyclo-spa.be

Other Riding

Given how busy the roads around Liège can be, there's a lot to be said for staying in one of the towns to the south of Wallonia's industrial and commercial centre. Remouchamps and Stavelot are good places from which to explore the many almost ghostly quiet roads through the Ardennes Forest. One of the best allows riders to tackle the most renowned of *La Doyenne*'s climbs without travelling too far south. It heads south out of Remouchamps, diving under the A26 viaduct and following the curves of the River Amblève. Continuing through Stoumont and towards Trois-Ponts, it is wonderfully peaceful, eerily so when the mist comes down and blankets the trees. Arriving at Trois-Ponts, you can either take the main N68 south a few kilometres to join the Liège route coming up from the south and take a left up and over the Côte de

ABOVE: Spring not only brings the professional peloton to this region, but also sees nature deliver a vivid display of life and colour.

Wanne, or follow the backroad towards Bergival, bearing left there to Rochelinval and emerging onto the N68 almost opposite the turn onto the Côte de Wanne.

In common with most of the Classics, the route of *La Doyenne* has changed many times over more than a century. Mont Theux and the Côte de la Vecquée are among a number of climbs that come in and out of the route depending on the organizers' whim.

The riding needn't all be climbing-focused, though. Wallonia's RAVeL (Réseau Autonome des Voies Lentes) offers 885 kilometres of paths and trails criss-crossing the region, one following the Meuse from its entry point into Belgium in the south all the way through to the Netherlands in the north, passing by Namur, Huy and Liège on the way. Full details of these routes are available on the RAVeL website (ravel.wallonie.be).

Stage ⑧
The Race at the End of the World
Lannilis–Lannilis, 204km [France]

The Tro Bro Léon has been called 'the Breton Paris–Roubaix', 'the Hell of the West' and 'the most beautiful race that you've never heard of'. Those first two descriptions give an idea of the kind of test it sets riders, but it's the latter that best encapsulates what this Breton one-day race is all about. Born out of one man's desire to foster the Breton language and culture, and held in late April when most of the cycling world is focusing on the Spring Classics, it takes place in French cycling's heartland in Brittany, the home region of five-time Tour de France winner Bernard Hinault, his long-time team director Cyrille Guimard and many other greats of French cycle sport.

The man behind it is Jean-Paul Mellouët, a passionate cycling fan and proud Breton. Searching, in 1984, for a way to fund the Breton-speaking schools in his hometown of Lannilis and inspired by the cobbled Classics, Mellouët and a few friends established a race for amateurs, the Tro Bro Léon, or Tour of the Léon, the western part of the department of Finistère. Run on farm and coastal roads in that rugged, frequently windswept region, its nod to Roubaix, the Tour of Flanders and other cobbled races came with the inclusion of several sections of *ribin* (the plural is *ribinoù*), the Breton word for any kind of unsurfaced road. In this case, the roads are gravel farm tracks, often with a strip of grass running down the middle, linking country roads.

'This course results in carnage. But it's beautiful as well. In fact, I really enjoyed it. It was like a really great mountain-bike ride.'

2015 winner Alexandre Geniez

While the comparison with Roubaix and the cobbled Classics is easy to make, the Tro Bro Léon offers a quite unique test. 'The approach to the *ribinoù* is similar to Roubaix but, as for riding them, it's more like cyclo-cross,' says Pierre-Luc Périchon, a member of the Breton Fortuneo-Vital Concept pro team. Although they are more akin to Tuscany's *strade bianche* than the cobbles of northeast France or Belgium, the *ribinoù* do have a rougher, more stony surface than the white roads of Italy. Consequently, racers tend to puncture far more often in the Breton one-dayer than they do in the Tuscan event. However, the more casual rider, who isn't racing in a pack and is better able to pick a line, should find the going a little easier on their tyres.

Following an anticlockwise loop based on Lannilis, 25 kilometres due north of Brest, the route heads south across the Aber Benoît, a wide inlet and quiet haven from the windy turmoil of the Atlantic. Turning west on the other side of the water at Tréglonou, where the squat houses built into the lea of the hillside closely resemble those of Cornwall and west Wales, the route runs parallel to the inlet. Continuing on to and quickly through Ploudalmézeau, the sense of proximity to Britain's west-facing Celtic regions becomes more apparent. The occasional clusters of trees in this 'Land's End' that takes the full force of the ocean lean eastwards, almost encouraging travellers to turn back, the prevailing wind often adding force to that sentiment.

BELOW: The Tro Bro Léon has been dubbed 'the Breton Paris–Roubaix' thanks to its use of a warren of farm tracks known locally as *ribinoù*.

However, the road beyond Kersaint-Plabennec reaches the sea and as it does so delivers the first hint of the beauty of this relatively unknown corner of Brittany. The little white-sand coves that dot the bay give way to rugged coastline when the road reaches the edge of the open ocean. After switching back inland to circumvent the Aber Ildut, the road ploughing between expanses of deep bracken, it weaves its way back to the sea again at Lampaul-Plouarzel for another brief seaside spectacular.

There are almost 100 kilometres and ten *ribinoù* to negotiate before the next sighting of the Atlantic. The first *ribin* arrives quickly, its passage unmistakeable thanks to a row of huge wind turbines running parallel. The *ribinoù* come thick and fast now as the route circles north of Brest via Milizac, Bourg-Blanc and Kersaint-Plabennec, where the rougher roads, with their grassy Mohican, burrow between hedges and crops. A 'no entry' sign stands sentinel at the start of most these sections. *Sauf riverains* – 'access only' – they declare, emphasizing how rough these seldom-used tracks can be, even when an attempt has been made in the past to surface them.

At Landerneau, the route moves north on one of the better sections of *ribin*. Three more that are less accommodating of tyre rubber send the route on a wide sweep around Le Folgoët, before continuing directly north for another rendezvous with the Atlantic. The road skirts the mudflats on the edge of Goulven Bay, diverts for a kilometre to trundle through Trégueiller on the 11th section of *ribin*, and arrows towards the coast at Ménéham. Farmland gives way to dunes and scrub dotted with huge, rounded boulders of light-brown sandstone, which bestow the beaches with sand of a creamy hue that helps to turn the sea wonderfully rich shades of blue on bright days. When the weather is less clement, however, this stretch is particularly exposed.

An old stone cross with patches of yellow lichen stands at the start of the 13th 'off-road' section, with a twin at the far end. Of course, it's only coincidence that this is the 13th, but it is pretty rough. The serious deterioration of what was once the sealed surface is the main reason for difficulty, as sections sit proud of the surrounding stones, creating sharp edges that are sometimes hard to see if there's any water on the road.

After switching back and forth southwards through the lanes and *ribinoù*, the 16th section turns the route west towards Lannilis and the finale. Approaching the outskirts of the town, you're almost home, yet 25 kilometres and several more bumpy sections of rough road still remain. They begin with a big loop around Lannilis to the sea, diving initially into high-hedged lanes and onto a *ribin* that leads up to and through the grounds of the Château de Kerouartz. The following section bores through the embankment supporting the main road above, via a corrugated concrete tunnel.

LEFT: Like Roubaix's cobbled roads or Tuscany's *strade bianche*, the *ribinoù* can be awfully dusty for those riding further back in the pack.

This quickly leads into another beautiful waterside stretch, weaving through the narrow streets of Aber Wrac'h, where the route turns sharp left (signposted Le Sémaphore) and down what initially appears to be a back alley. What starts as a lovely lane takes an uglier aspect as it passes an old convent. The green Mohican is back for *ribin* number 20. It persists on the next section, after which the route turns back towards Lannilis on the north shore of the Aber Benoît for what is, at 3.3 kilometres, the longest shake, rattle and roll of the day. Exiting it, Lannilis is just moments away.

Naturally, though, there are a few more meanders before the finish. Leaving Lannilis on the road south, the route runs straight for 700 metres, then switches hard left onto the final *ribin*, which twists left and then right underneath the trees to reach a smooth road back into town, where the finish is in Place Leclerc.

Hang on, though, two *ribinoù* remain... The Tro Bro Léon concludes with three laps on a five-kilometre circuit that features that last Meshuel section on each occasion. There's no real need to complete them, but as it may be a while before you're back at Finis Terrae, the end of the Earth, why not indulge?

Sportives

The organizers of the Tro Bro Léon have followed many of their peers by organizing a sportive version of their event the day before the professionals tackle the roads and *ribinoù*. The **Tro Bro Cyclo** offers two route options of 45 and 113 kilometres. Both start and finish in Lannilis, with the longer featuring 14 sections of *ribinoù* on a route that largely follows the second half of the pro course. The shorter version, which is open to mountain bikes as well as road bikes, includes six sectors of *ribinoù*. **Information:** www.trobroleon.jimdo.com/tro-bro-cyclo

The Grand Prix de Plumelec is another professional event that has also spun off into a different realm with a sportive. **La Morbihannaise Jean Floc'h Cyclosportive** is part of a weekend of racing in the passionate cycling town of Plumelec in southeast Brittany. Taking place in late May, the weekend (which begins on the Friday) features pro men and women's races, an amateur event and a women's World Cup race, in addition to the sportive, which is held on the Sunday. Offering three routes of 58.5, 103 and 159 kilometres, the courses all cover ground that has often featured in the Tour de France, including the tough ascent of the Côte de Cadoudal in Plumelec, which hosted the finish of the 2015 Tour's team time-trial stage. **Information:** www.grand-prix-plumelec.com

Brittany has produced many of the greats of French cycle sport, most notably five-time Tour de France winner Bernard Hinault, who hails from the town of Yffiniac, a few kilometres east of Saint-Brieuc. Taking place in mid-June, **La Bernard Hinault** is a sportive that pays tribute to the rider nicknamed 'The Badger', offering two very testing sportive routes and three rando-sportive routes that are far less taxing and where riders are not timed. All five options start and finish in Saint-Brieuc. The two sportives head east into the rolling countryside where Hinault used to train. The Arc-en-Ciel (Rainbow Jersey) version, commemorating his world championship victory, features 2,500 metres of climbing in its 195 kilometres, while the 120-kilometre La Martine, named after Hinault's wife, features 1,400 metres of vertical gain. The less competitive rando sportives measure 36, 80 and 120 kilometres. The former is open to families.
Information: www.labernardhinault.fr

Like Plumelec, the Breton town of Plouay celebrates its love of cycling with an extensive festival of events spread over four days at the end of August. The packed agenda features a men's world tour race, a women's World Cup race, a vintage bike festival and ride, BMX events and a wide range of sportive and *cyclotouriste* events under the **La Cyclo Morbihan** umbrella and catering for riders of all abilities. The two cyclosportives extend to

119 and 150 kilometres on rolling courses around Plouay.
Information: www.grandprix-plouay.com

Other Riding

Still one of the heartlands of cycling, Brittany often surprises because, despite the lack of big hills, its rugged terrain can prove very demanding. On the upside, the countryside is beautiful and wonderfully quiet, while that passion for two wheels means that cyclists receive plenty of respect on the road and a warm welcome away from it. There is good cycling in every part of the region, but the coastal roads are particularly impressive, especially along the English Channel coast in the north and facing out towards the Atlantic in the west.

BELOW: The wind can be a significant factor in such open countryside very close to France's Atlantic coast.
OPPOSITE: Looking down one of the rougher sections of *ribin*, with its grassy Mohican.

BELOW: This image perfectly captures the principal difficulties faced on the roads of the Tro Bro Léon – punctures and the wind.

Fact File The Race at the End of the World

Route Details

COUNTRY: France

RACE: 2015 Tro Bro Léon

ROUTE: Lannilis–Lannilis, 204km

TERRAIN: Slightly undulating dirt roads

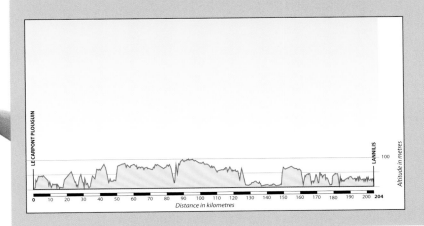

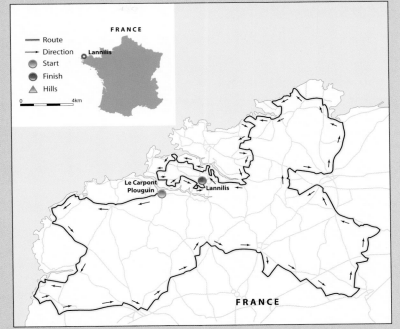

The Tour's First Climb

Gérardmer–Mulhouse, 171km [France]

'If you want spectacle, the Vosges is the best mountain range to deliver it. It's my favourite playground.'

Thibaut Pinot

1905's third edition of the Tour de France was the first to set the riders the challenge of tackling the country's mountain ranges. The Alps and the Pyrenees may be the best known of them in the modern era, but Tour boss Henri Desgrange initially considered those massifs far too taxing, and held off for another five years before he asked the Tour peloton to venture into the high mountains. Instead he sent them into the Vosges and specifically in the direction of the Ballon d'Alsace on the second stage of the 1905 race, which covered 299 kilometres between Nancy and Besançon.

Contemporary reports reveal that half a dozen riders reached the foot of the 12-kilometre climb in the lead group. Before starting up the climb, they swapped to bikes equipped with a gear better suited to the uphill test. Over the course of the next 40 minutes, the group was whittled down until it comprised 1904 Tour victor Henri Cornet, the only teenager ever to win the race, and René Pottier. Nearing the summit, Pottier edged clear of his rival. Writing in *L'Auto*, Desgrange describes Pottier as having 'his torso bent in two over the bars, his eyes fixed on the ground ahead, not easing up until he was almost at the top, at the moment when the large pines started to drop away on the other side of the climb.'

RIGHT: Like the Black Forest on the eastern side of the Rhine, the Vosges is criss-crossed by heavily forested mountain roads.

In the modern era, when stages finish atop high peaks, that effort might have been enough to secure Pottier a well-merited victory. However, almost 50 years would pass before the Tour introduced summit finishes, and the lightweight Pottier had the best part of 100 kilometres to cover to that day's finish. Ultimately the advantage he had eked out was not enough, as Hippolyte Aucouturier overhauled him and went on to win the day. Of much more significance, though, was the fact that the riders, averaging 18–20 kilometres per hour, had shown that they could cope with the particular challenge offered by the mountains, and that this terrain had actually enhanced the sporting contest. They have remained as an essential ingredient of the race ever since.

A century on from Pottier's symbolic achievement, the Tour paid tribute with a stage that encompassed the Ballon d'Alsace, but that also highlighted the extent to which the importance of the mountains has changed. There were no fewer than five categorized climbs before the Ballon d'Alsace, including the highest pass in the Vosges, the 1,338-metre Grand Ballon. Traversing the massif from west to east to finish in Mulhouse, the stage also emphasized the reasons why the Vosges is something of a forgotten paradise for cyclists. Its climbs are neither excessively long nor steep, while the roads are often beautifully quiet as they cut back and forth through dense forest.

Starting in the delightful lakeside town of Gérardmer, above which sits the ski resort of La Mauselaine – where Blel Kadri gave France its first stage win of the 2014 Tour de France – the route briefly follows the shore of Lake Gérardmer before cutting towards and over the Col du Haut de la Côte on the edge of the town. No sooner does it zip down off that first leg-warming climb than it dives into the forest and on to the first of the six categorized climbs, the Col de Grosse Pierre. The first of four third-category hills on that 2005 Tour stage – and the climb on which eventual stage winner Michael Rasmussen began his victorious escapade in 2005 – the Grosse Pierre is typical of the passes in the Vosges, topping out at a little less than 1,000 metres in altitude.

From there, the route shoots down into La Bresse, where it turns east and then northeast to climb the Col des Feignes sous Vologne. Beyond this very gently rising pass and the small ski resort of Belle Hutte, where *ski de fond* or cross-country skiing is the main attraction in these comparatively lowly mountains, the route cuts back on itself, weaving through the trees to the Col de Bramont.

Zig-zagging down through the hairpins from this summit, the route enters the Haut-Rhin department; ahead lies slightly more rugged terrain in the shape of the second-category Grand Ballon. Continuing through Wildenstein and along the eastern side of Lake Kruth Wildenstein, the going is very easy. But the turn onto the D27 signals a change, as the long (it's almost 22 kilometres) but shallow (it averages less than four per cent) ascent of the Grand Ballon begins.

After 15 kilometres of climbing, the road emerges from the trees and reaches Le Markstein, a small ski resort that can also be accessed via a much steeper road from Linthal to the east. Subsequently submerged by trees once again, the road drags steadily upwards to the Grand Ballon, which is topped by a radar station and offers a view that on clear days

extends almost 400 kilometres towards Mont Blanc, the Eiger and other lofty peaks in the Alps. Closer in are the Jura, Black Forest and Mulhouse, which is just 25 kilometres or so away as the crow flies.

Almost predictably, the route tracks a more errant flight path, running parallel to Mulhouse from the Col Amic, before turning completely away from the finishing city at Willer-sur-Thur. Almost imperceptibly at first, the N66 gains height as it runs along the Thur valley before kicking up very obviously for the fifth climb, the Col de Bussang.

At Saint-Maurice-sur-Moselle, the routes of the 1905 and 2005 Tour stages combine for the final ten kilometres of the Ballon d'Alsace. Sweeping back and forth through the forest, it's the ideal climb for most riders, especially those with five previous ones in their legs. The gradient is steady, rarely dropping below six per cent or edging above seven. Once your legs have found their climbing rhythm, sustaining that pace is not too taxing and the summit soon appears out of the trees. From the top, the route runs for 50 or so kilometres down into Mulhouse via Masevaux and Burnhaupt-le-Haut. Alternatively, a circular ride back to Gérardmer can be completed by turning back towards Saint-Maurice-sur-Moselle and tracking back north from there.

ABOVE: Spaniard Joaquim Rodríguez sprints towards a summit during the Tour's crossing of the Vosges in 2014.
OPPOSITE: The Tour peloton climbs through thick forest early on in the 2014 stage from Gérardmer to Mulhouse.

Sportives

The Alsacienne takes place just after the longest day, which may be just as well for riders tackling the lengthiest of its three routes. Dubbed 'The Indomitable', it covers 179 kilometres between the start in Cernay and the finish in nearby Hirtzenstein. Featuring Tour de France classics such as the Grand Ballon, Markstein, Firstplan, Petit Ballon and Platzerwasel, its shark-tooth route clocks up more a staggering 4,800 metres of climbing. The 137-kilometre Intrepid and 102-kilometre Audacious options are pretty full on, too. The route of the latter has a not too shabby 2,800 metres of vertical gain. **Information:** www.alsacienne.org

Part of the impressive Grand Trophée series, which features events right across France, **Les Trois Ballons** also takes place in June and features a lot of the roads and climbs that French Tour de France star Thibaut Pinot uses for training. Starting in Servance at the southern end of the Vosges and finishing in nearby Raddon-et-Chapendu, the event has two route options: the Gran Fondo is a huge 217 kilometres with more than 4,000 metres of vertical gain; the Medio Fondo extends to 105 kilometres. The three Ballons of the title are the Grand Ballon, the Ballon d'Alsace and Col des Chevrères, which is the main difficulty on the Medio Fondo route and is also known as Le Ballon de Belfahy. Pinot describes this area as being like the Basque Country, with lots of short passes about 5–8 kilometres in length. The Chevrères is among the most feared. 'It's a narrow forest road and the last four kilometres are very difficult,' Pinot says of it. **Information:** www.grandtrophee.fr/epreuve.php?C=22

The **Cyclosportive de la Planche des Belles Filles** is a relatively new event that has sprung up in the wake of the Tour de France's discovery of the vicious climb in this event's title. Chris Froome claimed the first stage to finish there in 2012, while Vincenzo Nibali reclaimed the race leader's yellow jersey when he won there in 2014 and went on to hold it all the way into Paris. Starting in Champagney and finishing on the top of La Planche des Belles Filles, a climb Pinot admits he's afraid of and has described as 'irregular and disconcerting', there are two route options of 130 and 86 kilometres. **Information:** www.tvs-vtt.org

Other Riding

Riding in Alsace and the Franche-Comté needn't be all about climbing. Sitting in the lea of the Vosges massif on the French side of the wide plain through which the Rhine flows, the Route des Vins runs for 170 kilometres from Marlenheim, near Strasbourg in the north, to Thann, close to Mulhouse. It passes through some of France's most beautiful villages and weaves its way between many of the region's most celebrated vineyards. Located at around the midway point on this stunning bike route, Colmar is the perfect place from which to explore it and experience some of region's most renowned climbs, which lie just to the west of the city. The Hautes-Vosges website (summer.hautes-vosges.net/circuits-de-cyclosport-hautes-vosges-summer.html) offers a wealth of information about circular rides across the massif, encompassing both road and off-road routes.

LEFT: Alsace is renowned for its white wines, and its vineyards provide a lush backdrop to the lowland riding here.

BELOW: The mountains in the Vosges are not on the same epic scale as the Alps, but the climbs come so often that riding there can be just as exacting.

Fact File The Tour's First Climb

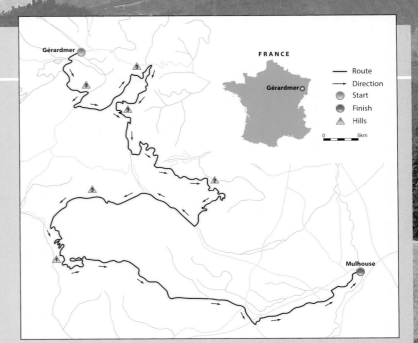

Route Details
COUNTRY: France
RACE: 2005 Tour de France (stage 9)
ROUTE: Gérardmer–Mulhouse, 171km
TERRAIN: Medium mountain

Climb Stats
Col de Grosse Pierre
HEIGHT: 955m
ALTITUDE GAINED: 199m
LENGTH: 3.1km
AVERAGE GRADIENT: 6.2%
MAXIMUM GRADIENT: 7.2%

Col des Feignes sous Vologne
HEIGHT: 922m
ALTITUDE GAINED: 277m
LENGTH: 9km
AVERAGE GRADIENT: 3%
MAXIMUM GRADIENT: 5.2%

Col de Bramont
HEIGHT: 956m
ALTITUDE GAINED: 221m
LENGTH: 3.4km
AVERAGE GRADIENT: 6.5%
MAXIMUM GRADIENT: 7.6%

Le Grand Ballon
HEIGHT: 1,338m
ALTITUDE GAINED: 788m
LENGTH: 21.9km
AVERAGE GRADIENT: 3.6%
MAXIMUM GRADIENT: 10%

Col de Bussang
HEIGHT: 731m
ALTITUDE GAINED: 279m
LENGTH: 6.2km
AVERAGE GRADIENT: 4.5%
MAXIMUM GRADIENT: 7%

Le Ballon d'Alsace
HEIGHT: 1,171m
ALTITUDE GAINED: 619m
LENGTH: 9.1km
AVERAGE GRADIENT: 6.9%
MAXIMUM GRADIENT: 8%

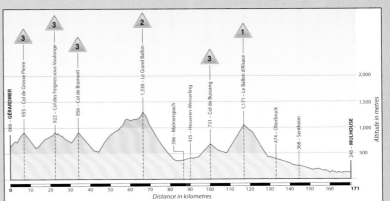

Stage ⑩
Black Forest Beauty
Singen–Feldberg, 177km [Germany]

Fact File Black Forest Beauty

Route Details
COUNTRY: Germany
RACE: 2005 Deutschland Tour (stage 7)
ROUTE: Singen–Feldberg, 177km
TERRAIN: Rolling, forest roads

Climb Stats
Notschreipass
HEIGHT: 1,120m
ALTITUDE GAINED: 736m

LENGTH: 13.5km
AVERAGE GRADIENT: 5.4%
MAXIMUM GRADIENT: 13%

Feldberg Pass
HEIGHT: 1,277m
ALTITUDE GAINED: 638m
LENGTH: 10.5km
AVERAGE GRADIENT: 5.8%
MAXIMUM GRADIENT: 10%

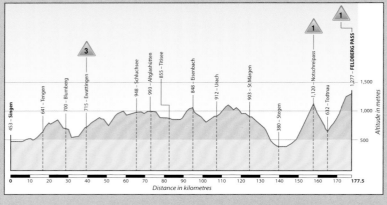

The Rhine valley bisects two outstanding cycling areas, one of them very well known, the other much less so. As the mighty river flows northwards from the spectacular falls at Schaffhausen, delineating the French–German border as it does so, mountain massifs rise up from the flat and fertile plain 20 kilometres either side of its waters. In France, to the west, is the Vosges, home to the Grand Ballon, the first mountain ever to feature on the Tour de France route. To the east, in Germany, is the Schwarzwald, or Black Forest, which is far more renowned for its unctuous gateau than the beauty of its roads.

However, as this stage of the 2005 Deutschland Tour clearly demonstrates, the Black Forest's heavily forested climbs are just as magnificent as the more famous ascents in the Vosges a mere 50 kilometres away. Indeed, the neighbouring ranges are almost mirror images of each other, their highest passes topping out at around 1,200–1,300 metres, with climbs extending to no more than ten kilometres in length and usually averaging less than six per cent. They are testing, but not to the point where riders are struggling so much they cannot admire the extravagant views across the Rhine to the smudge in the heat haze that is often the only sign of the Vosges in the thick humidity.

The ride begins in Singen, which lies at the top end of the Untersee, from which the Rhine begins its final passage towards the North Sea. This journey soon takes it over the spectacular falls near Schaffhausen, where the river, which is already 150 metres wide, drops 23 metres. The setting was described by writer Mary Shelley as 'exceeding anything I had ever seen before'. It really is quite something, especially when the river is in flood.

Heading west, parallel to the Swiss–German border, the route weaves between tree-capped hills and through rich farmland to Tengen. From here it hops over a small climb to reach Blumberg, at the heart of what is reputed to be one of Germany's most scenic areas. The small town at the southern edge of the Black Forest is surrounded by parks, forests, lakes and mountains. Continuing west, the route climbs again as it heads through the village of Ewattingen, site of a third-category King of the Mountains climb when the Deutschland Tour came through this part of the state of Baden-Württemberg.

After dipping into Bonndorf, the road climbs again and is swallowed up by the dense Black Forest for the first time. It reaches almost 1,000 metres in height before emerging from the thick greenery to reach the Schluchsee, Germany's highest reservoir and the highest lake in the Black Forest, and the waterside town of the same name. This is a hugely popular area for watersports, which will be very evident on hot summer days as the

OPPOSITE: The dense Black Forest offers a magically peaceful setting for riding.

route follows the north shore of the Schluchsee before cutting back into the forest and on to the tiny ski resort of Altglashütten, which lies in the municipality of Feldberg.

Just beyond, at Rotmeer, by turning left you can reach the foot of the finishing climb after only a handful of kilometres, but our route takes a right and begins a marvellous 100-kilometre loop through the forest to reach this same point. Within minutes it is running up the edge of another picturesque lake, the Titisee, which is surrounded on all sides by rounded, pine-covered hills. Passing through the spa town of the same name, the route climbs again to Eisenbach. Soon after, it turns west into the Urach valley.

A narrow corridor of farmland between trees that rise up onto the hilltops on each side, this is a lovely road, dipping initially, then rising again as the trees crowd right in at the verges. As the route turns north to Sankt Märgen, a spa town right in the heart of the Black Forest, it begins to descend, dropping steadily to start with, then much more quickly as it leaves Sankt Märgen. It slaloms wonderfully into Sankt Peter and then Stegen, which lies just a few kilometres to the east of the attractive city of Freiburg, which is an ideal base for circular rides in the Black Forest.

Turning south, the route dives back into the thick of the forest at Oberried. The road, which has already been rising gently for a few kilometres, kicks up a little more. It's only around four per cent for the next few clicks, but a big

right-hander soon after the left turn to Sankt Wilhelm delivers a more severe challenge. This is the toughest section of the 13-kilometre ascent of the Notschreipass. It was a first-category ascent in the Deutschland Tour, thanks principally to its final half-dozen kilometres, which average more than eight per cent and feature long stretches that are above ten.

Back in 1971, the Tour de France crossed this pass during a short stage between Basel and Freiberg, although it came at it from the much easier southern flank. Nevertheless, it says a good deal that Dutch mountain goat Joop Zoetemelk led over the top, for this is very much the realm of the specialist climbers, even though the wide and well-surfaced road might suggest otherwise.

From the summit by the Waldhotel and the Nordic skiing centre, the road plummets into the lovely little town of Todtnau, nestled beneath tree-covered mounts at the junction of three valleys. Swinging left into the valley heading east and, once again, gently upwards, brings the final challenge almost within sight. At Fahl, the road kicks up towards the resort town of Feldberg. Passing the Alpine Centre a little further on, it ramps up again, running in huge sweeping curves towards the resort town of Feldberg, which at 1,277 metres is the highest village in Germany.

It was as the race came out of these bends that Cadel Evans made a stage-winning attack on this first-category climb back in that Deutschland Tour of 2005, at the end of what had been a grim August day of rain and cold temperatures. To get one up on Evans, riders who have still got a little zip in their legs might consider taking the left turn in Feldberg up to the mountain of the same name that looms above it. The wide-open summit, very much a German equivalent of the Ballons now visible across the Rhine in the Vosges, tops out at 1,493 metres, making it Germany's highest peak outside the Alps. On a clear day, the view from this point is outstanding. To the west are the Vosges, to the south the Alps, to the north the Swabian Alps and to the east the Hegau volcanoes. It is one of those places where you feel on top of the world, especially when you've arrived by bike.

Sportives

The Germans are renowned for the occasionally excessive nature of their sportives, and this is ideally exemplified by the **Alb-Extrem**, which very necessarily takes place in late June when there's plenty of daylight. At 190 kilometres, the shortest or Classic route exceeds the longest in most sportives and racks up 3,000 metres of climbing. Next up is the Midsize route at a staggering 240 kilometres and an extra 1,000 metres

ABOVE: A steam train on the Wutach Valley Railway waits for the passage of the Deutschland Tour peloton when it tackled this stage in 2005.

RIGHT: Race jackets were *de rigueur* when the professionals tackled this stage on a damp and misty day in 2005.

of vertical ascent. Top of the range is Traufkönig, or King of the Trauf, the Albtrauf being the super-steep grades typical of the Swabian Jura around the small town of Ottenbach, to the east of Stuttgart, where the event has its HQ. This final option extends to a mammoth 300 kilometres with an astounding 5,400 metres of climbing. This is definitely one to work up to rather than plunge into as a sportive novice. **Information:** www.mrsc-ottenbach.de/index.php?id=103

Late September's **Rothaus RiderMan** comprises three stages taking place over consecutive days in and around the Black Forest town of Bad Dürrheim. It starts on the Friday with a hilly 16-kilometre time trial, followed by two hilly road stages that are around 100 kilometres in length over the next two days. This is a very popular amateur event that is part of the German Cycling Cup series that draws 30,000 riders across its ten events, which also includes the three-day Rad am Ring held at the Nürburgring motor-racing circuit in late July. There's also a kids' race on the Sunday, camping facilities and an expo. **Information:** www.en.riderman.de

The **SURM**, or Schwarzwald Ultra Rad Marathon, takes place in mid-September. Based in the Black Forest town of Alpirsbach, which lies around 50 kilometres east of Strasbourg and is famed for its brewery, it features some of the roads from the Deutschland Tour stage recreated above, but lies mostly to the north of it. The longest route of 230 kilometres has more than 4,000 metres of climbing, largely on beautiful and quiet forest roads. There are also 82- and 147-kilometre options. **Information:** www.surm.de

Riding in this region needn't be all about climbing. The long-standing **Bodensee Radmarathon** (The Lake Constance Gran Fondo), which also takes place in September, is essentially a flat ride around the lake. Taking in roads in Germany, Switzerland and Austria, the event has six different start locations and three route options: gold of 220 kilometres, silver of 150 and bronze of 82. Brilliantly organized, it also allows entry to under-16s if they are accompanied by an adult. At any other time of year, the 273-kilometre network of bike paths around the lake (www.bodensee-radweg.com) and as far west as the Rheinfall at Schaffhausen offers any number of ride options. **Information:** www.bodensee-radmarathon.ch

Other Riding

Starting and finishing in Freiburg, the 240-kilometre Southern Black Forest Cycle Route suits both riders who love hills and those who prefer to use the gradient to their advantage, as cyclists can catch a train up the most significant climb between Himmelreich and Hinterzarten. Taking in sights such as Wutach Gorge, the Petite Camargue nature reserve in France and the Southern Black Forest Nature Reserve, the route, which is mainly on asphalt paths that are virtually traffic free, also dips into Switzerland.

RIGHT: Like the Vosges massif on the opposite side of the Rhine, the Black Forest offers a 'medium mountain' test, with climbs topping out at an altitude of little more than 1,000 metres.

Stage ⑪
Water, Water Everywhere
Kiel–Hamburg, 220km [Germany]

Germany's links to cycling's biggest races go back to the sport's foundation. German ace Josef Fischer was the first winner of Paris–Roubaix in 1896 and was his country's main hope in the inaugural Tour de France of 1903. More recently, Germany was swept by cycling mania when Jan Ullrich, Erik Zabel and the magenta-clad riders of Team Telekom dominated racing towards the end of the 20th century. In 1996, as Ullrich fever began to grow, Germany's emergence as a cycling superpower was underpinned by the foundation of the HEW Classic in Hamburg, which became part of the ten-leg World Cup two years later. A year on from that, the country's national tour, which had not been run since 1982, was relaunched with the aim of becoming the fourth grand tour of the season.

By the middle of the first decade of this century, those highs had become very distant memories. The doping scandals that had bedevilled cycling hit Germany particularly hard when, just prior to the 2006 Tour de France, it was revealed that Ullrich had been working with infamous Spanish doctor Eufemiano Fuentes, who was found to be blood-doping several high-profile riders when caught in a sting operation carried out by Spanish police. While Ullrich never raced again, several of his illustrious peers were forced to admit that they too had been doping, resulting in T-Mobile, as Telekom were by then known, pulling out of the sport, the cancellation of the Deutschland Tour and, not long after, German TV ending broadcasts of the Tour de France.

This appeared to signal the end for the sport in Germany, but was instead just a distraction from a renaissance in which Hamburg's one-day race figured prominently. By now known as the Vattenfall Cyclassics, the port city's pro race had been underpinned by amateur events that attracted many thousands of riders. It was clear that Germany was embracing sportive-style events as fervently as it was shunning professional cycling. By embracing this enthusiasm, Hamburg's race survived and even thrived, to the extent that in 2015 more than 22,000 riders took part in the Vattenfall events, leading the organizers to claim its status as the biggest race in Europe.

The pro event remains on the elite level World Tour, alongside events such as the Tour de France and Paris–Roubaix. Although it has nothing like the same cachet as those races, it has always been highly prized, particularly among sprinters, to whom its flat course most obviously appeals. Sprint demons André Greipel, Alexander Kristoff and John Degenkolb are among the most recent victors, the former's success coming in the 20th edition in 2015, the anniversary marked by a radical change to the route. Previously based very much on Hamburg, with loops to the south and west as well as on a circuit within the city, the start was shifted to the port of Kiel. Located on the Baltic, 100 kilometres to the north, Kiel is Hamburg's partner in a joint bid to host the 2024 Olympic Games.

With Stena among the sponsors, the race actually rolled away from the deck of one of its ferries docked at the Schwedenkai terminal that

BELOW: There's water at almost every point on this route between the Baltic at Kiel and the River Elbe in Hamburg.

'The Vattenfall Cyclassics is the biggest race we have in Germany, it's like the Champions' League for us, and I would love to savour victory there in front of my home fans.'

André Greipel, prior to the 2015 race

links Kiel to Gothenburg. Weaving through the streets of the capital of the Schleswig-Holstein region, the route soon leaves the busy streets behind as it begins its move southwards to Hamburg.

With the Baltic at one end, the River Elbe at the other and numerous lakes in between, water is never far away. The route passes the Wellsee as it heads out of Kiel's southern suburbs, running directly towards Honigsee, on the edge of the lake that gives the neat village its name. Here it turns east and runs straight across the flatlands to Preetz, a pretty little town between the Postsee and Kirchsee. Skirting these in turn, then running on the narrow strip of land dividing the Scharsee and the larger Lanker See, the route makes a beeline for Plön, which is almost completely surrounded by water.

The route is barely into the town before it turns to head out of it, passing its 17th-century castle to reach Koppelsberg and then circling the western edge of the Grosser Plöner See, the biggest lake in Schleswig-Holstein. Thanks to its tree-lined shore and tidy towns, with marinas packed with leisure craft and launches ploughing back and forth across its waters, the lake is a peaceful haven, but seems busy when compared with the absolute tranquillity of the much smaller Stocksee, which arrives just a few kilometres later.

For the next few kilometres, as it arrows due south, the road passes farmland and gravel pits to reach the two Rönnaus, Gros and then Klein, and the waters of the Grosse Segeberger See. Weaving through the spa town of Bad Segeberg, the route runs close to the Kalkberg, a 90-metre-high gypsum outcrop that was significantly higher before centuries of mining took a toll on its altitude. Even so, it remains one of the loftiest features for miles around.

Switching to the west at Leezen, the route meanders through fertile agricultural land to reach the commuter town of Kaltenkirchen, just 20 kilometres north of Hamburg. Staying to the west of the port city, it continues through Quickborn and Pinneberg, the home town of Wimbledon

champion Michael Stich and the location of the beautiful baroque chateau, the Drostei, which is now a very plush restaurant. A few kilometres beyond, in the lively town of Wedel, the route reaches the north bank of the Elbe, one of central Europe's greatest rivers and still an important artery for trade and commerce into northern Germany and beyond.

Never losing sight of the Elbe for long, the route now heads directly into Hamburg, passing through the affluent suburb of Blankenese, where several outcrops provide impressive views over the river, among them the Waseberg. This is the key point for riders competing in the Vattenfall Cyclassics race. Rising through thick woodland that hides some of Hamburg's most exclusive properties, it only climbs to an altitude of 87 metres, but does so quite abruptly. After a switchback on the upper part, the gradient reaches 15 per cent as it passes under a footbridge.

The pros usually tackle the Waseberg three times, once on their first passage through Blankenese and then twice more after they have continued on to pass through the finish line. This lies in the centre of the city on Monckebergstrasse, one of the main shopping streets and the location of the spectacular neo-renaissance town hall, the Hamburger Rathaus. On this final section, the route runs along the infamous Reeperbahn, the port's red light district where the Beatles played in a variety of clubs in the early 1960s immediately before breaking through to become musical icons.

ABOVE: Little known by cyclists outside Germany, the state of Schleswig Holstein is criss-crossed by wonderful routes.
OPPOSITE: The speed of the Vattenfall peloton ensures that it is lined out as it hurtles through the finish heading into the final lap on the Hamburg circuit.

Fact File Water, Water Everywhere

Route Details

COUNTRY: Germany
RACE: 2015 Vattenfall Cyclassics
ROUTE: Kiel–Hamburg, 220km
TERRAIN: Flat

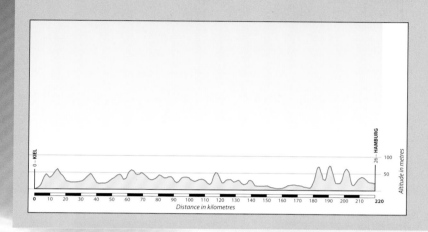

Route
Direction
Start
Finish
Hills

0   10km

BELOW: The 2015 Vattenfall peloton rolls away from the car deck of a ferry berthed in Kiel.

There could hardly be a larger contrast between this little stretch and the rather bucolic setting for most of what has gone before. Yet this underlines what makes this route special and explains why Hamburg's pro race has survived and, more particularly, why 22,000 amateurs turn out every year for one of the most popular events on the cycling calendar.

Sportives

The **Hamburg Cyclassics** brands itself as 'Europe's biggest race' thanks to a total of 22,000 riders racing against the clock on three different courses, measuring 55, 100 and 155 kilometres in length. The shortest course heads west from Monckebergstrasse, covering some of the same ground as the pros did in 2015. The intermediate route crosses Hamburg's spectacular Köhlbrandbrücke bridge for a loop in Lower Saxony that used to be part of the pro race prior to 2015, while the longest route combines both of these shorter options. The weekend also features Germany's

largest consumer bike fair and all manner of other bike-related activities. **Information:** www.hamburg-cyclassics.de

The German passion for cycling may not be very manifest at pro level, but it's absolutely unmistakeable for those who love a sportive. There are simply dozens of them in every region. The **NordCup-Radmarathon** comprises ten of the very best that are held in the north. Beginning at the end of April with the Rudi–Bode Radmarathon and concluding in early September with the intriguingly titled St Pauli Marathon To Hell, the events feature up to five different ride options. Three of the series – the RG Hamburg Radmarathon, the Rund um die Schlei and the Hollsteiner Wellenritt – also form part of the national RadmarathonCup Deutschland. **Information:** www.radsport-sh.de/nordcup-radmarathon.html

It may take place a good distance from Hamburg, but the **Velothon Berlin** does have a close link to the port city, or at least its professional race, as both

are owned by the same management company. Held in mid-June, the Berlin Velothon, which has sister events in Wales, Stuttgart and Stockholm, bills itself as Europe's second-biggest race, with more than 12,000 riders riding against the clock on courses of 60 or 120 kilometres that feature most of the German capital's principal tourist sights. **Information:** www.velothon-berlin.de

Other Riding

When completed, the Baltic Coastal Cycle Route will be Europe's second-longest bike route, extending to 7,890 kilometres on its journey through nine countries. Although the German section of the route has yet to be officially added to Euro Vélo 10, as it has been classified, more than 800 kilometres of coastal roads and trails already lie between Flensburg on the Danish border and Ahlbeck on the Polish frontier. With sandy beaches, rugged headlands and beautiful and bustling towns and cities, including UNESCO-listed Wismar and Stralsund, there is much to explore along

the Ostsee, as the Germans call the Baltic. To the north, Denmark offers another bounteous option, with 11 long-distance bike trails offering more than 10,000 kilometres of riding. In the midsummer months, when the weather is often idyllic, there can surely be few better ways to unwind than zipping along next to the sea and exploring one of the few countries in the world where the bike enjoys at the very least equal importance to motorized transport in terms of transport infrastructure.

ABOVE: The change in the Vattenfall Cyclassics route in 2015 meant that the route offered a brief glimpse of Germany's Baltic coast.

BELOW: The peloton contemplates the long climb that looms ahead in the Austrian Alps.

It was inevitable, given the constant push within sport towards tougher tests and, in theory at least, greater spectacle that professional cycling's peloton would eventually face the challenge of racing up mainland Europe's second-highest asphalted road to the Rettenbach Glacier, or Rettenbachferner, way above the Austrian resort town of Sölden. Although, at 12 kilometres, it is not especially long, its gradient and height more than offset this key factor when judging a climb's difficulty. Indeed, they do so to the extent that this is certainly one of the most taxing ascents in Europe.

The sport's best riders first took on that test during the Deutschland Tour in 2005, when American Levi Leipheimer was the first man to reach the lofty finish at 2,671 metres. Two years later, Spaniard David López, who later became a very solid mountain *domestique* at Team Sky, won there on the D-Tour's return. More recently, the 2015 Tour of Switzerland climbed to the Rettenbachferner. This provided Thibaut Pinot with the chance to reveal his form a couple of weeks before the Tour de France, where the Frenchman won the 'queen' stage at Alpe d'Huez, which tops out some 800 metres below the Austrian giant.

Oddly, the long-standing Tour of Austria has never ventured up this remarkable road, which some pros would undoubtedly suggest is the consequence of making best use of local knowledge. Located in the Ötztal Alps in the east of the country, the Ötztaler Gletscherstrasse, or Ötztal Glacier Road, was built in 1972 to provide access to ski stations on the Rettenbach and Tiefenbach glaciers. Anyone with a ski pass for these areas can use the road free of charge, but those without have to pay a toll for the drive up 2,830 metres. Only the road that climbs to 3,300 metres on the Pico Veleta in Spain's Sierra Nevada is higher. However, the Ötztal Glacier Road has a significant edge on the Veleta and most other ascents in the giant category, as it averages a lung-busting 10.7 per cent for its 12 kilometres of ascent.

The Professional Perspective

Welshman Geraint Thomas proved that he has the ability to compete with the best riders in the high mountains when he finished fifth behind Thibaut Pinot on the Rettenbachferner stage in the 2015 Tour of Switzerland, moving himself up to second place overall in the process.

'I didn't really know what to expect given how hard the climb was, and then with the altitude as well on top of that. It was certainly going into the unknown. I'd never raced up a climb like that before,' said Thomas.

'Your lungs are burning with the breathing. It is definitely different to going full gas at lower altitude. As soon as I crossed the line I was in proper oxygen debt and really hurting. You need a few minutes to get your composure again.'

The ride begins in Germany's most southerly town, Sonthofen, heading due east from there towards the Austrian border via the Oberjoch pass. The opening kilometres are easy enough, rising almost indiscernibly to Bad Hindelang. Just beyond the village the road changes from straight to meandering, swinging right initially and then weaving upwards at a steady rate through occasional woodland stretches. At 1,142 metres, the Oberjoch is not too severe, which was emphasized by its third-category status in 2007.

There is a small ski station at the summit. Not far beyond it, the road enters Austria on the long drop down to Weissenbach. For the next 20 kilometres, it runs through the bucolic setting of the Tannheimer Tal, a hanging valley that rolls constantly but very gently through pasture and small farming villages. After passing along the northern shore of the Haldensee, the road begins to drop into the Lech valley, reaching the river at Weissenbach and then following it northeast to Reutte.

Turning south to Lahn, the long ascent towards the Fernpass begins. This is one of the principal communication routes in this corner of Austria, and it can be busy with holiday traffic during summer months; there is an alternative way for those who want an extra dose of mountain mayhem before the Rettenbachferner (see 'Other Riding', page 105, for details). Climbing in a wide valley, the road goes back above 1,000 metres before scooting down into the attractive little ski resort of Lermoos, where the

view across the mountain meadows is dominated by Germany's highest mountain, the 2,962-metre Zugspitze.

Taking the L71 south leaves behind a good deal of the traffic. The serious part of the ascent to the Fernpass begins, too, although it's not overly arduous. Weaving its way up towards the summit, Fernpassstrasse rejoins the main route over the pass when this emerges from a tunnel just before reaching the Blindsee, which sits below the 1,224-metre summit. After a couple of wide sweeps downhill, the road schusses into Imst, where the autobahn collects the traffic on this side of the pass and leaves a quieter run alongside the River Inn before turning to Oetz, which sits in the shadow of the 3,008-metre Acherkogel.

Continuing south alongside the Ötzaler Ache, a favourite with whitewater rafters and canoeists that tumbles vigorously in the opposite direction, the road climbs steadily, emerging into another dramatic

ABOVE: Although the climbs are impossible to ignore, there is also lots of exceptional valley riding on this route.

OPPOSITE: Looking down towards the ten-kilometres-to-go banner on the lower reaches of the Rettenbachferner road, the effects of the gradient are clearly apparent as riders climb in small groups.

hanging valley at Winklern. Narrowing as it rises on this southerly course, the Ötztal valley passes resort after resort before reaching Sölden, once a remote village but now a winter sports centre that receives more tourists than anywhere else in Austria outside Vienna and Salzburg.

Just beyond the main lifts in the centre of the town, Gletscherstrasse cuts back from the main road. What's gone before has been a phoney war: now the real battle begins.

The first kilometre out of Sölden is far from intimidating, gaining height steadily as the road rises out of the ski village and up into the trees. However, when Ötzaler Gletscherstrasse cleaves off left from Innerwaldstrasse, the contest between cyclist and mountain turns ugly. The gradient is steady – steadily high, that is. It remains fixed at around 12 per cent and will remain that way for the next four kilometres. Like a balloonist who is desperately trying to gain altitude, cyclists could be forgiven for the urge to throw away anything weighty or unnecessary and take wing. Yet gravity and the gradient completely prevent that.

Emerging from the trees just short of the toll booth, the grade eases by five points, and the steepest part of the climb is done. 'Rettenbachferner is not fun,' tweeted Belgian pro Sep Vanmarcke, seeing a picture of himself at this point in 2015. As Vanmarcke hinted, a new kind of torment is about to commence...

With the River Rettenbach rushing by with icy melt water from the glaciers, the road straightens and ramps up three more per cent. For the next three kilometres the road is almost unwavering in its directness and steepness. As is the case on the topmost 'bald' section of Mont Ventoux, the final destination, a small cluster of restaurants and lift houses sitting beneath the grey-white bottom end of the glacier, is within sight yet appears to remain agonizingly out of reach. The landscape conspires to increase the torment.

Unlike majestic mountain roads that are designed to cater for every kind of vehicle and switch back and forth looking for ways to relieve straining engines, adding to the drama of a high-altitude setting as they do so, this is the ultimate in service roads. It runs straight and true up the side of the narrowing valley, with the aim of making access to the principal ski areas as rapid as possible. Now well above 2,000 metres and beyond the tree line, the view is unchanging, emphasizing the impression that little headway is being made.

A set of four switchbacks stacked one on top of the next finally offers a change of perspective and, on the widest sections of the corners, some easing in the gradient. Coming out of the last of them, the slope's severity falls a touch more, which is a relief given that the road has climbed above 2,500 metres. By now there's barely any greenery and the resort up ahead has an almost industrial aspect, with bare rock and rubble on all sides. Eventually, though, the landscape opens out. Over the last few hundred metres, as the resort finally offers itself up, there are superb views on all sides, particularly – and rather rewardingly – back down the valley towards Sölden. An even greater prize awaits those who swap bike for ski lift and continue up to the resort's highest point. On a clear day, there is an astounding panorama across snowy peaks and glaciers. It's a quite glorious finale to an epic day.

LEFT: With David López a few dozen metres ahead, Deutschland Tour leader Jens Voigt stands on the pedals as he nears the greying mass of the glacier at the summit in 2007.

> **'This is tougher than the cols in Italy and Mont Ventoux.'**
>
> Belgian ex-pro Wim Van Huffel

BELOW: Hard-riding Voigt's famous catchphrase was, 'Shut up, legs!'. Judging by his expression and that of Robert Gesink on his wheel, their legs' complaints are proving hard to ignore.

Sportives

It says everything about the **Ötztaler Radmarathon** that the course is ferociously tough and features so much climbing that very few professional race organizers would ever contemplate scheduling a stage along the same lines. An immense 238 kilometres in length, the route features four major passes, three of them more than 2,000 metres high – the Kühtai (2,020m), Jaufenpass (2,090m) and the Timmelsjoch (2,509m). Taking place in late August, starting and finishing in Sölden and limited to 4,000 riders, the event sells out very quickly. The winner usually finishes in around seven hours and is generally an ex-pro. Good amateurs take three hours longer. **Information:** www.oetztaler-radmarathon.com

While the Ötztaler Radmarathon may be extreme in terms of difficulty, the **Alpen Traum** is in a category somewhere beyond that. 'Traum' is the German word for dream, but it's hard to imagine anyone sleeping soundly with thoughts of this 252-kilometre ride that features 6,078 metres of climbing drifting around in their head. Starting at 6.30 on a mid-September morning in Sonthofen, it crosses the Oberjoch into Austria then follows pass after pass, including the toughest side of the Hahntennjoch, to reach Switzerland and then Italy via the Umbrail Pass. It continues on over the western side of the Stelvio and down the famous hairpins on its

eastern flank, before climbing one last time to the finish in Sölden, back in Austria. There are two easier options: the short route runs from the Austrian town of Landeck to Sölden and extends to 146 kilometres; the short route via Prad also begins in Landeck and is a mere 118 kilometres. **Information:** www.alpen-traum.com

Compared to these two monsters, the **Rad-Marathon Tannheimer Tal** looks quite benign and much more human. Taking place in mid-July and based on the town of Tannheim on the Austrian side of the Oberjoch pass, it offers three route options: the longest is 224 kilometres, the middle is 130 and the shortest a mere 85. The amount of climbing is far less severe, as well. The long route has a testing but not excessive 3,300 metres of vertical gain, while the two easier routes have less than 1,000. Covering much of the same territory as the northern part of the Sonthofen–Sölden stage, it's a beautiful ride through stunning upland valleys and over the occasional pass, none of which are especially lofty compared to the many giants in this vicinity. **Information:** www.rad-marathon.at

Other Riding

The most mountainous country in Europe, Austria offers a host of alternatives to those who can't resist the thrill of a big hill, particularly in this Tyrol region that lies in the very heart of the Alps. The key to enjoying the best of them is to avoid the passes that carry a lot of traffic, which on occasions would include the Fernpass on this stage route. In mornings, evenings and holiday periods this route can be a drudge for those on two wheels. To circumvent it, head southwest from Weissenbach, away from Reutte, and follow the Lech valley to Elmen. Forking left there, the road begins to climb rapidly, but eases as it leads to Bschlabs and Pfafflar, where the amazing Hahntennjoch pass begins.

A favourite among local cyclists, it also has a reputation as one of the more perilous roads in the Alps, that danger stemming mainly from the mudslides that can sweep across it in bad weather. Averaging only a touch below ten per cent for the final five kilometres to the top, where the road often clings to the cliff face, there are sections of almost twice that as the road climbs quickly through several hairpins, tunnels and the occasional rock arch. Wild, rugged and magnificent, it tops out at 1,894 metres, then hurtles down through scree and boulder fields to Imst.

Fact File Europe's Highest Stage Finish

Route Details
COUNTRIES: Germany, Austria
RACE: 2007 Deutschland Tour (stage 5)
ROUTE: Sonthofen–Sölden, 157.6km
TERRAIN: High mountain

Climb Stats
Oberjoch
HEIGHT: 1,150m
ALTITUDE GAINED: 330m
LENGTH: 8.5km
AVERAGE GRADIENT: 3.9%
MAXIMUM GRADIENT: 9%

Fernpass
HEIGHT: 1,211m
ALTITUDE GAINED: 230m
LENGTH: 7.4km
AVERAGE GRADIENT: 3.1%
MAXIMUM GRADIENT: 5%

Rettenbachferner
HEIGHT: 2,671m
ALTITUDE GAINED: 1,294m
LENGTH: 12.1km
AVERAGE GRADIENT: 10.7%
MAXIMUM GRADIENT: 14%

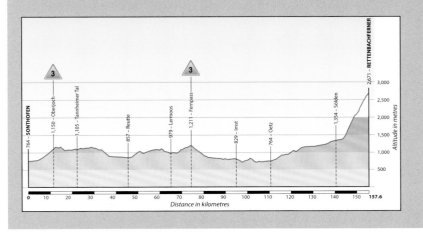

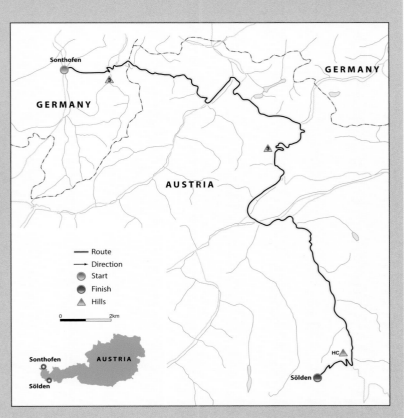

To the Foot of the Eiger

Bellinzona–Grindelwald, 171.4km [Switzerland]

BELOW: As a lone rider nears the top of the Susten Pass, the peaks behind are lit up by the late-afternoon sun.

'The Susten Pass gets my vote as the best descent in the sport, because coming down off there is where I got to my fastest ever speed on a bike – 108 kilometres per hour!'

Maurizio Fondriest

The beauty of riding in the Swiss mountains is that most of the roads appear to have been designed with the cyclist in mind. Although many of them soar to altitudes in excess of 2,000 metres, they generally do so in comparatively leisurely style. They sweep upwards in huge, extravagant curves, suggesting as they do so that Swiss road engineers consider a gradient greater than ten per cent vulgar and rather unnecessary, as something they would prefer to leave to their peers over the border in France, Austria and, above all, Italy. Taken from the 1999 edition of Switzerland's national tour, this route emphasizes both the elegance of this approach and the way in which it can tempt riders of all abilities onto some of the Europe's highest roads, encouraging access rather than laying down a challenge.

It begins in the spectacular setting of Bellinzona, capital of the Italian-speaking Swiss canton of Ticino. Lying a few kilometres from the northern extent of Lake Maggiore, Bellinzona holds World Heritage status thanks to the Castelgrande, Montebello and Sasso Corbaro castles, which dominate the town. Setting out from the northern side of the Castelgrande, the ride tracks the River Ticino on route two. This can be busy in rush hour, although the north–south A2/E35 motorway, which also tracks the Ticino, sucks up most of the traffic.

At Biasca, the route, which has been rising almost indiscernibly since the start, forks left into a narrower valley, where the Ticino, the motorway, the main railway line and our course get squeezed in more tightly together. Just beyond Giornico, the river begins to flow with urgency, signalling an increase in the gradient on what is now the Via San Gottardo, the first step towards the fabled St Gotthard Pass. Approaching the climb, the motorway and railway keep vanishing into tunnels. At Airolo, they disappear altogether, boring through the mountain for 17 kilometres.

A main road continues over the pass, but don't make the mistake of following the road traffic as you will miss one of the most astonishing sections of road in Europe. At the foot of the climb, a sign diverts cyclists off to the right onto the Via Tremola, which winds to the 2,091-metre summit via 38 hairpins. Stacked up one on top of the next, like the folds of a drawn curtain, the bends instantly capture the eye. However, the wonder of the St Gotthard Pass is not these swirling switchbacks, but the road's surface, which is cobbled all the way to the summit.

Built in the first half of the 19th century to ease passage through one of the most important trade routes in the Alps, the Via Tremola was superseded initially by the main road and then by the motorway tunnelled through the mountain. But the desire to enable through traffic to travel more quickly has been to the benefit of the old road. Sections that had been covered with tarmac have been restored, the flat-topped cobbles renovated or replaced. The result is a unique and totally glorious experience, far smoother than the roads of the cobbled Classics in

BELOW: The cobbled Via Tremola up to the St Gotthard Pass is generally accepted as one of the most beautiful mountain roads anywhere in the world.

northern Europe. Brilliant engineering also extends to the gradient, which remains between seven and nine per cent apart from one short section three kilometres from the top, when it briefly goes above 11.

Climbing towards the top of the pass, the curving patterns of the cobbles and the tufts of grass sticking between the stones cause the road to almost blend in with the rocky landscape and scree fields, suggesting that nature has somehow laid this perfect trail. At the summit there are a couple of hotels and restaurants on the edge of Lago della Piazza. Beyond this little lake, the cobbles continue for three kilometres along the Strada Vecchia before the old and newer roads combine, entering the German-speaking canton of Uri on the descent towards Hospental.

This tidy village overlooked by a crumbling 13th-century tower offers a wealth of delights to mountain lovers. Having zipped down from the St Gotthard, a turn to the west here leads onto the Furkapass, while the route north leads quickly to Andermatt, which lies at the foot of the Oberalppass. Continuing on towards Göschenen, the road dives into the Schöllenen Gorge, a precipitous cleft where the Teufelsbrücke, or Devil's Bridge, leaps across the rushing Reuss. Legend has it that construction of the original bridge was so tough that the devil offered to complete it in exchange for the soul of the first being to cross it. The locals agreed but chased a goat across the finished bridge, angering the devil, who returned with a huge stone to destroy it, only to abandon it when confronted by an old woman brandishing a cross.

At Göschenen, the motorway and railway emerge from the St Gotthard tunnel and run alongside the route as far as Wassen, where the latter forks left and northwest onto the first ramps of the Susten Pass. At almost 18 kilometres, this is the longest ascent on the route, is consistently demanding and, particularly over the final half-dozen kilometres, is breathtaking in both senses of the word.

After the long drop from the top of the St Gotthard, it's a sudden shock for the legs to be climbing again, and quite steeply, too, on the road out of Wassen. But this is quite different mountain scenery to the St Gotthard. Tracking up the northern flank of the valley above the waters of the Meienreuss, it follows a straight course running directly towards the Wendelhorn and the Fünffingerstöck, with its five jagged peaks. The head of the pass is visible from some distance away, which can be daunting as progress towards it is not rapid, but the scenery is fabulous, with more peaks and glaciers appearing as the road climbs. Beyond 2,000 metres, the road switches southwest towards the Stein Glacier and soon reaches the short tunnel at the summit that leads through into the canton of Berne and on to the close-to-30-kilometre descent into Innertkirchen.

Built over seven years up to 1945, the Susten Pass was the first in Switzerland built purely for road traffic rather than following a long-established trading and travel route. Thanks to this, it's beautifully surfaced and engineered. After a few hairpins just below the summit,

OPPOSITE: Riding high on the Grosse Scheidegg Pass, with a majestic mountain backdrop.

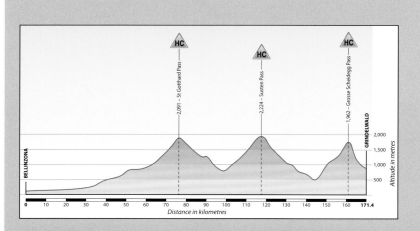

Route Details
COUNTRY: Switzerland
RACE: 1999 Tour of Switzerland (stage 5)
ROUTE: Bellinzona–Grindelwald, 171.4km
TERRAIN: High mountains

Climb Stats
St Gotthard Pass
HEIGHT: 2,091m
ALTITUDE GAINED: 932m
LENGTH: 12.7km
AVERAGE GRADIENT: 7.3%
MAXIMUM GRADIENT: 11.4%

Susten Pass
HEIGHT: 2,224m
ALTITUDE GAINED: 1,308m
LENGTH: 17.4km
AVERAGE GRADIENT: 7.5%
MAXIMUM GRADIENT: 9%

Grosse Scheidegg Pass
HEIGHT: 1,962m
ALTITUDE GAINED: 1,262m
LENGTH: 16.4km
AVERAGE GRADIENT: 7.7%
MAXIMUM GRADIENT: 12.5%

it flows like a giant slalom course down the mountain. There are long straights and most of the corners are so well cambered that the brakes need merely a touch. Professionals have been known to achieve speeds in excess of 110 kilometres per hour on these slopes, although amateurs should always bear in mind that the pros are racing on closed roads.

The left turn at Innertkirchen leads on to the Grimsel Pass, another spectacular climb. But that's for another day. Instead, the route continues on towards Meiringen, veering left before the town towards the Grosse Scheidegg. This is another long and quite gruelling climb, so it could well be time for a break. Just a few metres up the climb, there's an ideal spot for a rest in the form of the Reichenbach Falls. Renowned as the location of the final confrontation between Sherlock Holmes and his arch enemy, Professor Moriarty, the falls have a combined drop of 250 metres, the awe-inspiring plunge of the Upper Reichenbach accounting for almost half of that.

Back in the saddle, the narrow road climbs alongside the cascading River Reichenbach through thick woodland and past occasional farms. Thanks to a bar on all motor traffic except postal and farm vehicles, it is wonderfully quiet. The lack of traffic does mean that the road surface is not as well maintained as the Susten's, but that is not a critical issue going upwards. Thankfully, the descent off the other side into Grindelwald is not in the same dilapidated state, as it is a public road.

Emerging from the trees and into a hanging valley, the gradient eases considerably. Dead ahead is the Schwarzenwaldalp, its lower peak half concealing the upper part of the mountain as the Rosenlaui Glacier hangs over its shoulder. The road steps again to a slightly higher level and passes the Hotel Rosenlaui, before kicking up much more steeply at the start of the final run to the summit. Much of the next seven kilometres is wickedly steep.

After one final wooded section, the ribbon of a road ventures on into lush mountain meadows, running parallel to the course of the Reichenbach which runs towards the cliffs on the south of the valley, the glacier above feeding it with meltwater throughout the summer months. Approaching the summit, the peaks on the other side of the pass begin to come into view, including the Eiger, its infamous North Face almost permanently in shadow.

Once over the top of the Grosse Scheidegg, the shorter but steeper western route can be covered in a fraction of the time taken to ascend its eastern flank. Within half an hour you can be sipping a beer in a Grindelwald café and making a start on replenishing your carb levels, all while taking in one of the most world's most celebrated mountain vistas.

RIGHT: Climbing into fabled mountaineering country with Grindelwald and the Eiger not too far distant now.

Sportives

For a rather sedate experience of the St Gotthard Pass, nothing can top the **Gran Fondo San Gottardo**, which takes place in late July. It offers three routes, of 42, 57 and 110 kilometres, each of them starting and finishing in Ambri, just a few kilometres down the Ticino valley from Airolo. They all begin with the cobbled ascent of the St Gotthard. The two shorter routes return on the main road down the pass, the middle route wiggling through the hills above Ambri before the finish. The longest option continues over the St Gotthard to tackle the 2,429-metre Furkapass and the 2,478-metre Nufenenpass to serve up more than 3,000 metres of vertical gain. **Information:** www.granfondosangottardo.com

Naturally, there are events right at the far end of the difficulty scale, too. Among the best known is the **Alpen Brevet**, which takes place in late August. Based on Meiringen, it gives riders the choice of three routes: the silver crosses three passes and extends to 132 kilometres; the gold takes in four

and covers 172; and the platinum crosses five passes during its staggering 276-kilometre jaunt. The passes are slightly different on each. The gold route, for example, is the only one that includes the St Gotthard, although all three cross the Grimselpass and Susten Pass. By the way, the vertical gain on the platinum is 7,031 metres. Ride it and weep! **Information:** www.alpenbrevet.ch

The **Highway to Sky** event in Innertkirchen stands out for a number of reasons. For a start, assuming the elements are collaborating, it takes place on closed roads. Secondly, it's a time trial. Thirdly, it is only 28 kilometres long. It takes place in mid-May and sets competitors the challenge of riding to the summit of the Susten Pass against the clock. As the pass does not usually open until well into June, there is little public traffic on the road, and what traffic there is gets blocked until the cyclists have all set off for the summit. Leaving at 20- to 30-second intervals, competitors climb 1,606 metres to the top.
Information: www.highwaytosky.com

Other Riding

One of the beauties of riding in this part of Switzerland is the ease with which circular routes can be put together featuring anything between two and half a dozen celebrated climbs. Innertkirchen is an ideal base for an adventure of this kind, as there are major climbs in every direction. Andermatt is a good option, too. The most obvious loop from either town is a circuit taking in the Grimsel, Furka and Susten passes. Substituting the Nufenen for the Furka enables you to add the Via Tremola route over the St Gotthard as well.

Another way to include the St Gotthard from Andermatt is to head east over the Oberalppass and then south over the Lukmanierpass to reach Biasca, then return north up the Ticino valley to Airolo and over the St Gotthard. The Grosse Scheidegg doesn't fit in with these loops so easily, but it is such a wonder and its two sides are so different that few will be disappointed at riding it in one direction, then returning in the other.

BELOW: From the top of the Grosse Scheidegg Pass, a dirt road rises even higher into the wonderland of soaring peaks and glaciers.

Romandie Double-Cross

Marly–Les Diablerets, 185km [Switzerland]

The switch in focus between the one-day Classics and cycling's major stage races begins in late April and early May with the Tour de Romandie, a five-day test of time trialling and climbing form that takes place in French-speaking Switzerland around Geneva and Lausanne. In recent seasons, both Bradley Wiggins and Chris Froome have used victory in Romandie as a stepping stone towards success in the pre-eminent stage race, the Tour de France.

This stage comes from 2013, when Froome emerged as Team Sky's standard-bearer for the Tour. Already leading the race going into the 'queen' stage between Marly and the resort town of Les Diablerets, Froome extended his advantage despite bad weather forcing the organizers to shorten the route. They had scheduled for the peloton to tackle the fearsome Col de la Croix by two different routes, but heavy snow scuppered this plan. The decision to trim off the second ascent of

the Croix made very little difference to Froome, however, as the Briton still scattered his rivals. Only Simon Spilak was able to stay with Froome, the Slovene taking the stage win as Sky's leader rolled in behind him with the race all but won going into the time trial on the final day.

As most of the high-mountain passes are still closed when the Tour de Romandie takes place, the organizers had to send snowploughs over the Col de la Croix to clear a route through the drifts. In fact, the Croix, which forms part of ski and luge runs during the winter season, is usually closed until late May. But it remains open until November, giving cyclists a large window of opportunity to tackle this impressive pass.

Starting in Marly, in the mainly French-speaking canton of Fribourg, the route initially heads into the German-speaking canton of Bern to reach Giffers, where it turns to the southwest. At Le Mouret it joins the Route de la Gruyère, which runs through the heart of the region that produces the world-famous hard, yellow cheese that is traditionally a key component of the *croque monsieur*, the toasted ham-and-cheese sandwich that is a staple of French menus.

Rising continuously but only very slightly, this dead straight road offers an ideal warm-up as it runs between lush, green pasture ripe for munching by the cheese-producing livestock. Beyond La Roche, the route reaches Lac de la Gruyère. It's towards the bottom end of this reservoir that the

first indications of some serious climbing ahead start to appear. Hills emerge, and then high peaks beyond them.

Running close to the River Sarine and a one-track railway line, the going remains easy until Montbovon, where the road begins to rise and weave to reach Rossinière and Les Moulins, which marks the start of the first notable test. At 1,445 metres, the Col des Mosses is not in the giant category and, at a touch more than four per cent, its average gradient is hardly nightmarish either. But it's quite long and merited first-category status in Romandie and second category when the Tour de France came this way heading for Verbier in 2009.

It ascends in two large steps, the first, and more severe, coming immediately. After two kilometres of climbing through the trees, the road emerges onto a plateau, which continues for four kilometres to the village of L'Étivaz, where the second four-kilometre, tree-lined step begins. This

ABOVE: As the Romandie peloton rides through lush farmland, snowy high-mountain peaks begin to emerge on the horizon.
OPPOSITE: With the flat riding in the valley behind them, the peloton tackles the early ramps of the day's serious business on the climbs.

BELOW: Vineyards aren't a feature that would usually be associated with the Swiss Alps, but there are plenty of them on the south-facing slopes in this region, even at quite lofty heights.

reaches another plateau, where the resort of Les Mosses sits. From here the road sweeps down on a perfect surface to Le Sépey. Rather than continuing on towards Aigle, home of the International Cycling Union's HQ, it veers away to the east and Les Diablerets, the ride's ultimate finish location and the obvious start point for those looking for a shorter route option.

The nature of the road leading up the north flank of the Col de la Croix gives a clear warning that this is a much more serious climb than the last. It is far narrower, its surface is rougher and the gradient is tougher. It is also much more open, and offers expansive views in all directions as it climbs quickly away from Les Diablerets. The vistas take a little of the edge off the grade, which eases off significantly beyond the little resort of Les Mazots, 1,500 metres from the top.

The descent quickly becomes steep, which is worth remembering as the route returns this way after looping over the Pas de Morgins. This circuit begins at Villars, where the route swoops down to the Rhône valley at Ollon as the river heads towards the eastern end of Lake Geneva. It tracks upstream for a few kilometres before angling across it near Bex and then continues to Monthey, where the ride's third climb begins.

Like the previous two, the Pas de Morgins was rated a first-category summit in Romandie. Following the Vièze, a tributary of the Rhône that comes tumbling down in the opposite direction, this pass is pretty straightforward until the road comes out of the hairpin bends above Troistorrents and takes a more direct path towards France, which lies on the other side of the summit. This is one of the quieter routes between the

> 'The stage was a sentimental journey around some of the roads and slopes where I had trained when I went to the UCI school in Aigle as a naïve young kid out of Africa.'
>
> Chris Froome

two countries and that's to its advantage, although it doesn't compare at all with the Col de la Croix in terms of majesty. Indeed, the descent back to Troistorrents on the Route Forestière on the other side of the valley is more impressive.

After swooping through Troistorrents, Monthey and back over the Rhône into Bex, the most testing examination of the ride begins. This southern flank of the Col de la Croix is very long, extending to more than 22 kilometres. It begins in uncomplicated fashion, but that all changes as soon as the Route de Gryon forks left and upwards at Bévieux. The gradient more than doubles, averaging close to ten per cent for a couple of kilometres as it winds up through dense deciduous woodland that gives way to rows of vines stacked one upon the next climbing the mountainside to Fenalet, where the slope eases off a degree.

Above Fenalet, the vines give way to verdant pasture, over which there are wonderful views across the valley that continue as the road ascends into Gryon, a mid-sized resort that has managed to keep much of its original charm and avoid the ugly over-development that has blighted so many Alpine ski stations. Above it lies the bigger resort of Villars, home to two of the most expensive of the renowned Swiss boarding schools and the location of the junction that leads back up towards the Col de la Croix.

Beyond the sudden bustle of Villars, peace quickly returns, but so too do steeper grades, although the added exertion is offset by glimpses of the Mont Blanc massif. Three kilometres from the pass, the road ramps up savagely, or at least it is likely to feel that way after 20 clicks of upward effort. The gradient remains stuck at ten per cent almost to the top, where the twin glaciers of the Diablerets massif are among the spectacular sights that can be seen. On a warm day, what better reward could there be than a few minutes' recuperation to take all this in before the short drop into Les Diablerets for something more physically restorative.

Sportives

Held in the northern part of the Romandie region, the **Wysam 333** was established in 2002 by Samuel Wyss, the father of long-time BMC Racing professional Danilo Wyss, who won the Swiss national title in 2015. There's a very obvious clue to the daunting test facing participants in the event's title. Extending to 333 kilometres and held in late June, the mostly rolling course features three large loops based on Orbe, the home town of the Wyss family. Riders set out at 4.30am with the goal of completing the course before 7.30pm. For those who either don't fancy the 333-kilometre option at all or decide they don't when they're already under way, there are 111- and 222-kilometre alternatives. Event ambassador Danilo Wyss comments: 'The Wysam 333 is an extraordinary challenge that you have to prepare for months in advance, both physically and psychologically. After 250 kilometres, motivation and the desire to finish the 333 kilometres have to suppress fatigue, because from that point everything depends on what's going on in your head.'
Information: www.wysam333.ch

Initially established as the Pascal Richard Cyclosportive in tribute to Switzerland's 1996 Olympic road-race champion, the **Gruyère Cycling Tour** covers much of the same ground as the 2013 Tour de Romandie stage. Organized by the same company as the Swiss stage race and taking place in early September with the town of Charmey as the start/finish point, it offers two route options. The longer, extending to 115 kilometres, crosses the Col des Mosses to Les Diablerets, then continues over another Romandie regular, the Col du Pillon, and finally the 1,633-metre Col du Mittelberg. The shorter 76-kilometre option features the latter of these three passes.
Information: www.gruyere-cycling-tour.ch

Featuring half-a-dozen Swiss pros as ambassadors, including FDJ's Steve Morabito, the **Cyclosportive des Vins du Valais** runs up one side of the Rhône valley from Sion and returns down the other, passing many of the Valais region's prime wineries on the way. It takes place on 1 August, Switzerland's national day, and offers four route options. The longest, the Varen, measures 130 kilometres and the shortest, the Riddes, 37 kilometres. In between these two are the Lens at 98 kilometres and the Fully at 65. There are three timed climbs on the Varen, the longest of them being the 12-kilometre climb up to Lens. Following the event, there are festivities to celebrate the national holiday, including concerts and fireworks.
Information: www.lacyclosportivevalaisanne.ch

Other Riding

In addition to Switzerland's central position in Europe, good communications and low taxes, professional racers have long been attracted to the country by the variety of riding it offers, from long, flat valleys to high mountains and everything in between. French-speaking Romandie is a microcosm of this. To the north lies the Three Lakes area, where 2011 Tour de France champion Cadel Evans spent several years living. Based near Mürten, the Australian relished the quietness of the roads in the rolling terrain to the west of Berne. To the south, heading towards northern Italy, there is a host of high passes and resorts, including Verbier, where Alberto Contador all but wrapped up the 2009 Tour de France title, and Crans Montana. In the west, overlooking Geneva, are the mountains of the Swiss and French Jura, which are often overlooked by cyclists. Comparable in size and their forested aspect to the Vosges, the Jura's almost secret roads are very well worthy of a diversion from the Alps.

RIGHT: The Romandie peloton begins to thin out as the gradient ramps up and the pace at the front goes the same way.

Fact File Romandie Double-Cross

Route Details
Country: Switzerland
Race: 2013 Tour de Romandie
Route: Marly–Les Diablerets, 185km
Terrain: High mountains

Climb Stats
Col des Mosses
HEIGHT: 1,445m
ALTITUDE GAINED: 562m
LENGTH: 13.7km
AVERAGE GRADIENT: 4.1%
MAXIMUM GRADIENT: 8%

Col de la Croix (north flank)
HEIGHT: 1,776m
ALTITUDE GAINED: 613m
LENGTH: 8.4km
AVERAGE GRADIENT: 7.3%
MAXIMUM GRADIENT: 12%

Pas de Morgins
HEIGHT: 1,279m
ALTITUDE GAINED: 854m
LENGTH: 13.0km
AVERAGE GRADIENT: 6.6%
MAXIMUM GRADIENT: 10.5%

Col de la Croix (south flank)
HEIGHT: 1,776m
ALTITUDE GAINED: 1,351m
LENGTH: 22.6km
AVERAGE GRADIENT: 6%
MAXIMUM GRADIENT: 10%

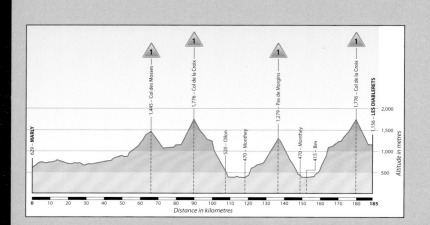

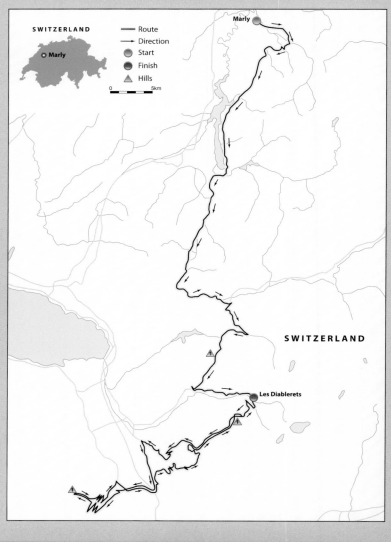

Cycling's Greatest Climb

Chamonix–Alpe d'Huez, 184.5km [France]

BELOW: Looking down from Alpe d'Huez, the Tour de France's racers can be seen climbing through the village of Huez with the town of Bourg d'Oisans in the valley below.

The Professional Perspective

'It's always great to go back there. It's become a pilgrimage point for most cyclists, which makes it fun. When I'm on bike tours with my company I love riding my bike slowly and enjoying the view, but I would have to say it's the least scenic mountain that I see over months at a time. I love coming down the Col de Sarenne on the far side of it, but all I can say about the route up is that it's a good road to get to a ski area. I think it's a pretty dull climb. Sure, there's all the history of it, but in my mind it's more of a cycling stadium than a beautiful road through the gorgeous French Alps. It's really at its best when all of the spectators are on it to see the Tour go by. It really is out on its own then.' 1992 Alpe d'Huez winner Andy Hampsten

Professional cycling's link with ski resorts dates back to the early 1950s, when race organizers realized that winter sport venues not only offered a physical test for riders but could also provide a lot of empty beds for a big race looking for accommodation options. Subsequently, many ski resorts have looked to cycling not only as a way of boosting out-of-season takings, but also as a marketing tool and as the foundation for summer-season activities. No resort has made a greater success of this than Alpe d'Huez, which is one of France's four leading ski domains and also has an international reputation as the greatest climb in cycling.

The 13.8-kilometre ascent from Bourg d'Oisans is not the toughest, nor the most attractive climb in the Alps. However, thanks to the masses that throng its slopes when the Tour de France heads towards it, it has become the most iconic and the climb that the professionals describe as the most thrilling to race up. That popularity stems from the regularity of the Tour's visits. After what appeared destined to be a one-off visit to the Alpe in 1952, the Tour eventually returned in 1976 and has ventured back again on another 27 occasions. To a large extent, the bond between race and climb that blossomed from the mid-1970s was the result of Dutch fans flocking to the Alpe. They came initially because Dutch riders kept winning at the resort, but also because the Alpe d'Huez stage quickly turned into a reason for cycling's biggest party.

Between 1976 and 1989, Dutch riders won eight times in 13 visits to the Alpe. The run started with Joop Zoetemelk, but this second success in 1977 was more notable, both because of the profile of the stage and the way in which it unfolded. It followed what is the classic route when approaching Alpe d'Huez from the north, crossing the Madeleine and Glandon passes to arrive in the Oisans region. The stage itself saw ace climber Lucien Van Impe ride away from his rivals on Glandon to what seemed a certain victory on the day and in the overall classification, only to crack half a dozen kilometres from home. He then got run over by a race official's car and lost all hope of glory, while race leader Bernard Thévenet rode out of his skin to save the yellow jersey after Dutchman Hennie Kuiper had triumphed at the summit.

That 1977 stage set out from the swish resort of Chamonix, which is tucked in beneath the northern edge of the Mont Blanc massif. It's a spectacular setting, the wide valley guided westwards towards Geneva by towering cliffs on both sides, the shotgun cracks of the Bossons Glacier resounding as the road passes the downhill runs at Les Houches. The route takes a dive here, meandering back and forth under the autoroute. At Saint-Gervais, another past start point for this iconic stage, it climbs consistently for the first time, topping out at Megève. It drops steadily from there, reaching the valley floor at Ugine and then tracking the River Arly into Albertville.

Swinging east and then south, the route rises little by little heading up the Isère valley before cutting across this river at Feissons, where the real climbing instantly begins. At 1,993 metres, the Madeleine is a relatively high pass, but it's its length and the constant changing of the gradient rather than its altitude that take a toll. Extending to 25 kilometres, this is a climb that even the top pros fear as it tends to highlight any sign of physical weakness, eating away at the rhythm of racers who want to maintain a steady pace. It plays into the hands of the mountain goats, who are able to accelerate rapidly on its steeper ramps and recover a little when it eases up before speeding off again.

It rises through dense woodland to begin with, winding up through the trees so that you can rarely see more than 200 metres ahead, effectively breaking the climb down into short and easily achievable sections. Occasionally, the greenery parts to allow views across the Isère valley. Traffic is light, as it is far quicker to take the main and autoroutes around the base of this Vanoise massif that sits between the Isère and Maurienne valleys.

After half a dozen kilometres, the gradient begins to ease and, beyond the hamlet of Villard-Benoît, the road descends for a kilometre or so. This opportunity to recover is good in the short term, but comes with obvious consequences. The climb is only a third done, and its average is now revealed as being rather skewed. Approaching La Thuile, at about the ascent's halfway point, the road kicks up, not too severely to begin with,

LEFT: The steepest sections of the climb to Alpe d'Huez come early on as the road spirals quickly up from the valley floor.
OPPOSITE: The desolate beauty of the upper part of the Glandon Pass.

but then with real venom. As the woods give way to scrub and pasture, the vista opens up, too, offering glorious views in all directions as the road switches back and forth, negotiating streams and gullies.

The penultimate in a series of less arduous steps is the prelude to the final four kilometres to the summit of the pass. The first three average almost nine per cent, but the gradient is easing off considerably by the time the cluster of buildings at the crest come into view, among them the Banquise restaurant. The sign on the summit announces 'Col de la Madeleine, Altitude 2,000m' in an understandable attempt to put it alongside lofty giants. However, the 1,993-metre pass is so magnificent that it doesn't need this artificial boost.

The road off the far side of the Madeleine into the Maurienne averages eight per cent and barely varies from that all the way down into the valley. It's open, with long straights at the top, and fairly rockets down into the resort of Longchamp. Below here, there are more switchbacks with long straights between them. The second half of the descent is through woodland – beware of damp spots under the trees – arrowing through them to La Chambre on the valley floor. After this exhilarating downhill, the road hops across the River Arc, flicks through some roundabouts and begins to follow its tributary, the Glandon, which flows down from the eastern edge of the Belledonne massif.

To a large degree, the western sides of the Glandon and Madeleine mirror each other. Topping out at just below 2,000 metres, they rise steadily through woodland early on, have a section that is almost flat in the middle and then rear up quite savagely towards the summit. The differences between them are small but significant. The Glandon is a little shorter – but don't read that as a reason to go at it a touch harder, because the final two to three kilometres feature what are consistently the steepest grades anywhere along this route.

After ten quite taxing kilometres, the gradient relents at Villard-Martinan. In the midst of this respite, the little ski village of Saint-Colomban-des-Villards provides the last chance of refreshment before the summit. Not far beyond it, the increased urgency in the flow of the Glandon is a sign that the road is rising up again, as the trees give way to scree fields running down from the peaks and rock faces above. The gradient goes up another couple of points passing through meadows filled with wildflowers. Then, above Le Sappey, the brutal finale begins. Looking up, the top is evident, but folds in the landscape hide several hairpins before the summit. Climbing through them, riders get a fabulous view back down the pass before hauling up onto the small plateau at the summit.

Just a couple of hundred metres over the top, there's a chance for refreshment at the restaurant that sits on the corner where the Glandon and Croix de Fer passes split. From there, it's a fast run down one of the most stunning valleys in the Alps, passing the waters of the Grand Maison reservoir. A wicked dip halfway down cuts momentum suddenly, but once out of it the road zips on through the trees to emerge on the edge of the large Verney reservoir. The road crosses the dam at the end, switches down into Allemond and soon crosses the Romanche to reach the D1091 main road between Grenoble and Briançon.

This road is busy but has a wide shoulder to accommodate the large numbers of cyclists, most of them drawn by the famous climb that is starting to become evident on the cliff face on the far side of the valley, across the Romanche. Weaving through Bourg d'Oisans, the road jumps over the river and runs straight towards this cliff face, veering left at the last moment and immediately onto one of the steepest sections of this fabled ascent.

The climb of Alpe d'Huez has 21 hairpins, which are numbered backwards from that figure. The first five, which take the road very quickly up to the church at La Garde, are unusual. The stretches between them are hard going, while each corner is like a little landing, providing respite at the top of a flight of stairs. However, these almost flat sections are killers for riders who prefer to find a rhythm and stick to it. Legs strain, then spin frantically, then strain again. Above La Garde, maintaining a steady pace is easier.

ABOVE LEFT: Aussie Adam Hansen grabs a beer from a fan as the Tour riders negotiate the mayhem at Dutch Corner on Alpe d'Huez.
RIGHT: The resort of Alpe d'Huez is just a few pedal revolutions away for Eritrean rider Daniel Teklehaimanot.
OPPOSITE: The tightly packed Montvernier hairpins immediately gained iconic status when they featured on the route of the 2015 Tour.

The second church on the climb comes into view at bend seven. Set just below the neat little village of Huez, this is 'Dutch Corner', a place of merriment and mayhem when the Tour passes through and where the kerb stones are permanently a shade of orange. Above Huez, the hairpins are set wider apart as the road rises through the meadows and ski fields immediately below the resort of Alpe d'Huez. The gradient is a touch steeper, too, making the final kilometres hard going. But once up to the shops and restaurants in the main street, the hardest parts are done. All that remains is to sweep around the tourist office and up to the un-numbered 22nd hairpin, then it's a quick scoot down to the Avenue Rif Nel and the sharp left turn up to the finish of the sport's most legendary climb, with the Grandes Rousses massif towering majestically above.

Sportives

One of the oldest and most popular of sportives, **La Marmotte** sets out from Bourg d'Oisans and completes a huge circuit of the Grandes Rousses–Galibier massif before returning to Bourg and heading up to Alpe d'Huez to finish. It takes place in early July, but its 7,000 places sell out many months before that, so getting a place in it is the first hard task to be completed. On the day, the route includes the Glandon, Télégraphe and Galibier passes. With the addition of the Alpe, that means more than 5,000 metres of climbing. It's an extremely hard test, and the organizers have recognized

this by setting up a two-day alternative, the Rando Marmotte, which halts overnight in Valloire, the resort in the saddle between the Télégraphe and Galibier. **Information:** www.marmottegranfondoseries.com

Taking place the weekend before La Marmotte and kicking off the Trophée de l'Oisans, a week of events that includes that sportive and culminates in a time trial up Alpe d'Huez, **La Vaujany** offers two route options. The longest, at 173 kilometres, features the climbs of the Grand Serre, Col d'Ornon, Alpe d'Huez and the wild and very wonderful Col de Sarenne before finishing the short but steep run up to Vaujany. The 109-kilometre option misses the loop over Alpe d'Huez and the Sarenne. **Information:** bike-oisans.com/en/events-cycling-mtb-oisans/la-vaujany-oisans-trophy

St-Jean-de-Maurienne has become a Mecca for cyclists searching for a variety of high-mountain challenges. Sitting close to the Madeleine, Glandon, Croix de Fer and Galibier passes to name just the most renowned, the town is also the starting point for August's **Cyclosportive de la Madeleine**. Its three routes feature the Madeleine but tackle it in quite different ways. The shortest 70-kilometre option rolls for 50 kilometres to La Chambre and then delivers the full-on Madeleine experience. The 100-kilometre route crosses the Col de Champ-Laurent and Col du Grand Cucheron passes prior to the Madeleine, while the longest 127-kilometre alternative offers something

very different and quite special. After the Champ-Laurent and Grand Cucheron, it continues on to the Col de Chaussy, which begins with the truly astonishing Lacets de Montvernier, 17 tiny hairpins stacked one on the next over just three kilometres. Made famous by a debut appearance in the 2015 Tour de France, they should be near the top of every rider's to-do list. **Information:** www.cyclosportivelamadel.wix.com

The well-established and popular **Time Megève Mont Blanc** sportive takes place in early June. Its three routes start in Sallanches and trace the same route initially, crossing the Colombière and Aravis passes. The 85-kilometre option then turns towards Megève, while the longer 111- and 144-kilometre routes continue on to the Col des Saisies, the former crossing this once before heading into the finish while the latter completes a second passage over the Saisies. **Information:** www.csportsmegeve.com

BELOW: Team Sky set the pace for their yellow-jersey-clad race leader Chris Froome on the flat valley road leading to the foot of Alpe d'Huez.

Other Riding

The French region of Savoie offers enough climbs and route options to fill a lifetime of riding opportunities. The best way to start is to pick a town to use as a base and go out exploring from there. On the northern section of this route, Annecy and Megève are ideal options, as both offer lots of accommodation and rides to suit all levels of ability. There are cycle paths around the beautiful lake at Annecy and more testing options on all sides, including the monstrously tough 2013 Tour summit finish at Semnoz.

The difficulty on the north side of the Madeleine is finding circular routes and avoiding the traffic on the N90 valley road that runs to Bourg-St-Maurice and on to the major resorts of Tignes and Val d'Isère. However, for those looking to bag Tour de France climbs, Moûtiers is a decent option as it lies within easy reach of Courchevel, Méribel, La Plagne, Les Arcs and Val-Thorens, as well as the Madeleine.

To the south of the Madeleine, St-Jean-de-Maurienne is the ideal choice. Sitting at the foot of the Croix de Fer, Mollard and Chaussy passes, it's also very close to the Galibier and Glandon. Over in the Romanche valley, meanwhile, Bourg d'Oisans is the perfect place from which to tackle not only Alpe d'Huez, but many more striking and often more beautiful climbs around it. Among these are the two sensational 'balcony' rides that branch off from the climb up to Alpe d'Huez. One runs north from Huez through the traditional and unspoiled ski resort of Villard-Reculas; the other heads south from La Garde towards another small ski centre at Auris-en-Oisans. Both feature knee-trembling sections cut high into the sheer cliff face hundreds of metres above Bourg. The more sedate ride up the Col d'Ornon is also recommended and offers a little-known surprise. Take a right a couple of kilometres up the Ornon in the direction of Oulles, and you'll find yourself on a Montvernier-like set of hairpins that end in that village.

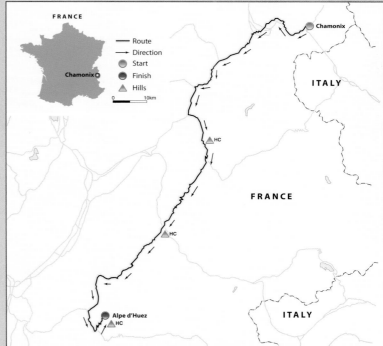

Fact File Cycling's Greatest Climb

Route Details
COUNTRY: France
RACE: 1977 Tour de France (stage 17)
ROUTE: Chamonix–Alpe d'Huez, 184.5km
TERRAIN: High mountain

Climb Stats
Col de la Madeleine
HEIGHT: 1,993m
ALTITUDE GAINED: 1,543m
LENGTH: 24.5km
AVERAGE GRADIENT: 6.3%
MAXIMUM GRADIENT: 11.3%

Col du Glandon
HEIGHT: 1,924m
ALTITUDE GAINED: 1,472m
LENGTH: 21.4km
AVERAGE GRADIENT: 6.9%
MAXIMUM GRADIENT: 12%

Alpe d'Huez
HEIGHT: 1,860m
ALTITUDE GAINED: 1,116m
LENGTH: 13.8km
AVERAGE GRADIENT: 8.1%
MAXIMUM GRADIENT: 13%

Note: The profile length reflects the full ride today, including any section of neutralised riding that would not have been counted as part of the official race.

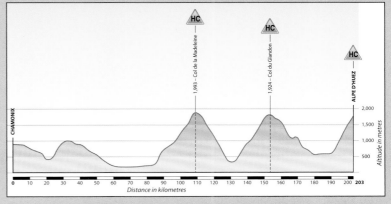

Stage 16
In Pantani's Wheeltracks
Merano–Aprica/Valtellina, 195km [Italy]

ABOVE: Not far short of 3,000 metres high at its summit, the Stelvio Pass is susceptible to bad weather at any time of year.

OPPOSITE: The upper sections of the Stelvio are kept open by snowploughs, creating huge snowbanks at the roadside.

Although Marco Pantani bagged his first professional victory 24 hours before this stage of the 1994 Giro d'Italia, his status as one of the sport's legendary climbers has its foundation in this epic day over two of the race's most iconic summits – the Stelvio and the Mortirolo. Pantani later admitted he didn't know much about the Mortirolo before he raced up it, although he had been told it suited his qualities as the most spring-heeled of specialist climbers. The rider dubbed *Il Pirata* ('The Pirate') softened his rivals up on its precipitous slopes before delivering a sabre-like victory thrust on the final climb of the Valico di Santa Cristina. In his wake, he left a trail of devastated riders, notably defending champion and

five-time Tour winner Miguel Indurain, whose hopes of retaining the title had been shattered.

This ride commences in Merano, which lies in the German-speaking South Tyrol region of Italy. Heading east on the Strada del Passo dello Stelvio up the Vinschgau, the fertile upper part of the River Adige valley, the route passes the apple orchards and vineyards for which this area is renowned. This road, which goes on to cross the Reschenbachpass into Austria, can be busy, although those who want to avoid the traffic can escape onto the Vinschgau bike path that runs parallel to but often some distance from the highway.

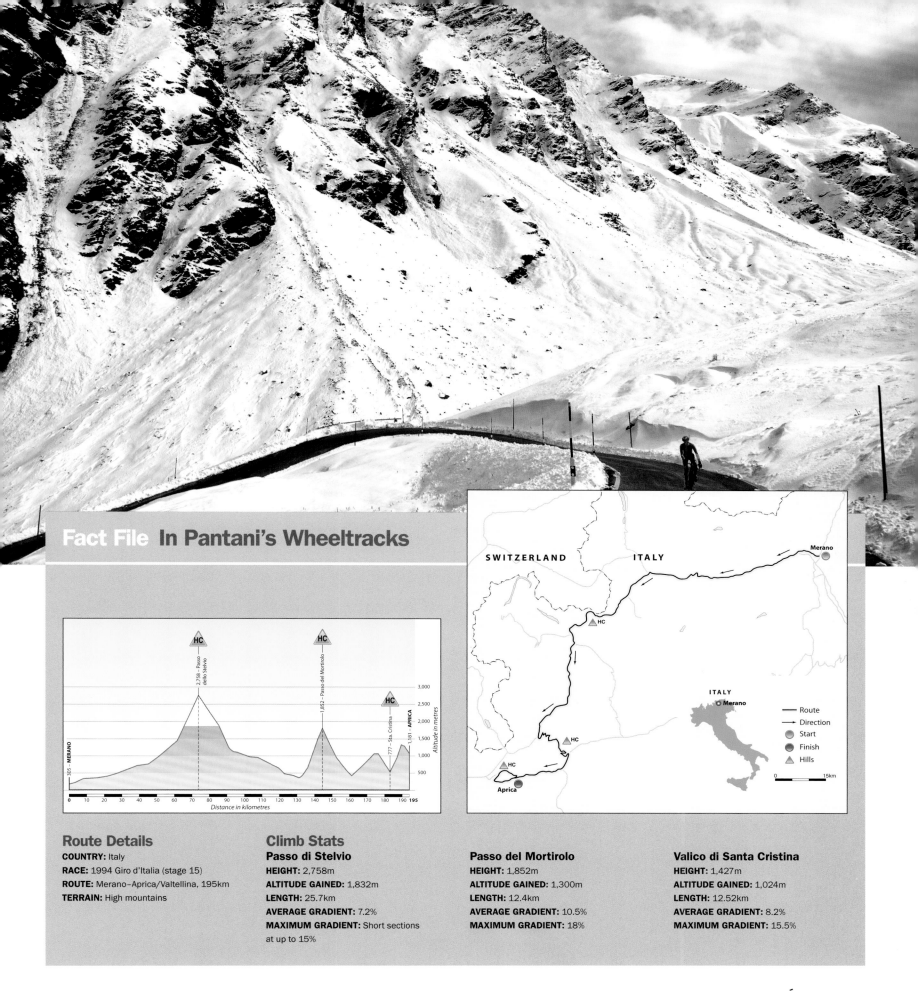

Fact File In Pantani's Wheeltracks

Route Details
COUNTRY: Italy
RACE: 1994 Giro d'Italia (stage 15)
ROUTE: Merano–Aprica/Valtellina, 195km
TERRAIN: High mountains

Climb Stats

Passo di Stelvio
HEIGHT: 2,758m
ALTITUDE GAINED: 1,832m
LENGTH: 25.7km
AVERAGE GRADIENT: 7.2%
MAXIMUM GRADIENT: Short sections at up to 15%

Passo del Mortirolo
HEIGHT: 1,852m
ALTITUDE GAINED: 1,300m
LENGTH: 12.4km
AVERAGE GRADIENT: 10.5%
MAXIMUM GRADIENT: 18%

Valico di Santa Cristina
HEIGHT: 1,427m
ALTITUDE GAINED: 1,024m
LENGTH: 12.52km
AVERAGE GRADIENT: 8.2%
MAXIMUM GRADIENT: 15.5%

'The Mortirolo is a terrible climb... it's perfect for a mountain bike. On the hardest parts, I was riding a 39x27 and I was hurting, really hurting. It's the hardest climb I've ever ridden.'

Lance Armstrong

BELOW: It's not easy to give an idea of a climb's gradient in a photo, so this image speaks volumes about how tough an ascent the Mortirolo is.

Most of the traffic and almost all of the trucks disappear when the Strada del Passo dello Stelvio bears off to the left at Spondinig, making a beeline for Prato allo Stelvio, then continues towards the pass on a road built up above the roiling waters of the Suldental. The river's often frantic progress in the opposite direction is an obvious indication that the long climb of the Stelvio is now under way, although the change in gradient is not too radical for the moment. However, the appearance of huge, snow-capped peaks sealing up the top end of the valley suggests that some serious climbing is not too far distant.

The change comes in Trafoi, where huge, tidily stacked piles of wood outside every building attest to the harshness of the winters in this village, which sits surrounded by huge peaks at an altitude of 1,300 metres. The road rises straight through the village until it meets the Schöne Aussicht/Bella Vista Hotel directly in its path and rebounds off this establishment into the first of four-dozen hairpins. For the next 17 kilometres, the gradient will remain above seven per cent, and sometimes well above.

This incredible road owes its existence to the desire of the Habsburgs to construct a route between Lombardy and the Vinschgau. Designed to encourage trade and, particularly, to ease military movements in this high-mountain region that was long a part of the Austro–Hungarian empire, the road was designed by Carlo Donegani. The Brescia architect has been fêted for this exceptional feat of engineering ever since. A Mecca for car drivers, partly thanks to BBC's *Top Gear* voting it 'the greatest driving road in the world', the Stelvio is equally popular among those on two wheels. Motorcyclists gleefully slalom up and back down its slopes, often startling cyclists so rapid is their approach.

Both flanks of the pass are impressive, but the classic ascent is this eastern side, which features 48 of the Stelvio's 75 hairpins. Initially the road climbs through pine forest, the trees creating a barrier that on a quiet day often leaves cyclists in a haven of peace, the only sounds their breathing and the whirr of chain over sprockets. These interludes allow those who are dependent on leg- rather than horsepower the opportunity to reflect on the brilliance of Donegani's creation, which enables altitude

BELOW: One of the 48 hairpins on the eastern flank of the Stelvio, most of which are stacked one upon the next as the road snakes up the mountainside above Trafoi.
OPPOSITE: Trafoi quickly becomes a distant memory as bend after bend lifts the road high above the village.

to be gained with relative ease and compensates to some degree for the prolonged effort required to achieve the summit.

As at Alpe d'Huez, the hairpins are numbered in reverse order. Initially there is some distance between them, but bend 42 brings a change. Sweeping right around it you're onto the first 'ladder' of switchbacks, although the density of the trees cloaks this marvel of engineering. The road rises quickly to reach bend 35, which sits about a thousand vertical metres below the summit. By the next gaggle of hairpins, beginning at bend 32, the trees are starting to thin out, allowing stunning views across to the Ortler massif on the southern side of the valley. Climb a little further and the Franzenshöhe hotel and restaurant comes into sight and, high above it, there's a first glimpse of the top of the pass.

Looking down from the summit at the highest 20 or so hairpins, you could be forgiven for thinking that they were something from a child's drawing of a fantastical mountain road. It really is that wonderful, and seeing that view will be ample reward for negotiating those final bends, which lift the road from 2,188 metres at the hotel to more than 2,700 metres at the summit.

The strain of riding at this kind of altitude can make this section into a bit of a breathless slog, but there is good reason to relish the next half-dozen kilometres. For a start, the gradient does ease a little above the Franzenshöhe. It also helps that from bend 14 onwards the hairpins are heaped so compactly, the rock and stone walls above one switchback supporting the lower part of the next, that the top of the pass is not only very evident but almost seems to come more quickly than expected.

The last few bends are among the steepest on the mountain, but by that point the thrill and relief of knowing you've just about made it kicks in. At the top there are cafés, restaurants, hotels, a bank, a surprising number of shops selling tacky mementos and, often, lots of motorcyclists high-fiving each other having managed to make it to the top aboard high-powered machines. It feels slightly surreal to arrive in this busy little hub having climbed so high through a landscape where just about the only sign of man's incursion has been the incredible road. It does, though, mean you can reload with something warm while you drink in that view and dwell for a few minutes on what is a crowning achievement for any cyclist.

From the summit, the road plummets past the Swiss border post and the turn onto the Umbrailpass towards the ski resort of Bormio. Although less

ABOVE: A monument to legendary and ill-fated Italian climber Marco Pantani at bend 11 on the Mortirolo, a climb that rose to prominence thanks to his feats.

numerous than on the other flank, there are still hairpins aplenty, interspersed with longer, straighter sections. After he had tied up the 1980 Giro on this stage, partly thanks to the daredevil descending of teammate Jean-René Bernaudeau, Bernard Hinault admitted that he'd feared for his wellbeing on these extremely fast sections, where unlit tunnels add a significant element of danger.

Just before Bormio, a left turn heads up the equally impressive Passo di Gavia. But those set on an encounter with the Mortirolo will continue through the stylish resort on the SS38 for another 30 kilometres, where a rather nondescript left turn at Mazzo di Valtellina heads away from the valley floor and into trees that conceal the first vicious ramps of the Mortirolo, also known as the Passo di Foppa.

There are no fewer than 33 hairpins on this gruelling ascent, some going with the precipitous incline rather than attempting to take the edge off it. Between kilometres two and nine, the gradient is north of 12 per cent, suffocating enough even without trees crowding in on both sides of the narrow ribbon of a road, cutting off any hint of a cooling breeze and often shutting out any view that might offer even the most temporary distraction from this gruelling test. Although the late Marco Pantani (whose feats on this climb are commemorated at bend 11) dismissed any rider who used anything more than a 23 sprocket, it's wise to opt for something much bigger, a 27 at least. As you twiddle towards the summit, ponder on where doping's excesses took the sport and riders with turbo-charged blood around the turn of the millennium.

Between bends five and four, with the gradient already easing, the pines finally give way to rough pasture, which continues to the summit. Unlike the majesty of the Stelvio Pass, this is a very unremarkable point and there's little incentive to dawdle before the far less precipitous drop

into Monno and Edolo. Climbing once again as it continues on through Aprica, the road's final test is the Valico di Santa Cristina.

Although far less exacting than the Stelvio or Mortirolo, it should not be underestimated, especially for those who have already had these two monsters gnawing savagely at their reserves. The average gradient may be a more palatable eight per cent, but this is a pass of two halves. The first, on the main SS39 road, is steady. However, just before this road switches south and down into the Valtellina, the route swings right onto the Via Maranta, heading for the hamlet of Mezzomonte, and takes on a quite different complexion.

This narrow road, which hasn't featured on the Giro's itinerary since 1999, is tightly tree-lined, often mossy and damp, and is seriously steep. Climbing in this muggy, sometimes cloying realm, where traffic is almost non-existent, it is not easy to summon up the hysteria that greeted Pantani when he flew up these slopes in 1994. His exploit more than doubled the TV audience, from three million watching as the stage crossed the Stelvio to more than seven million by this point. A cycling legend was born on these slopes, although you would never guess that from the very discreet brown sign at the Santa Cristina's summit.

For those wanting to loop back towards the Valtellina, the road from the pass towards Trivigno and onwards leads back to the top of the Mortirolo. Otherwise, follow the drop down into the resort town of Aprica, which is fast and should be taken with care given the dampness under the trees, to complete what is sure to be an unforgettable day's riding.

Sportives

The **Granfondo Stelvio Santini** takes place in early June. Established in 2012, it has already become a favourite for sportive-baggers as its longest 151-kilometre route features both the Mortirolo and the Stelvio. The three route options all start in Bormio and finish atop the Stelvio, tackling this epic ascent from the Bormio side. The short and medium versions don't include the Mortirolo, which some may regard as a good reason for missing the longer option, but if you've come this far... **Information:** www.granfondostelviosantini.com

At the end of August, the Passo dello Stelvio Park authority closes both sides of the Stelvio to motorized traffic, enabling riders to have what is effectively a pro-like closed road over one of Europe's highest passes as their playground. The descent off the Umbrailpass into Switzerland is also closed, which allows participants in the **Stilfserjoch Radtag** (the Stelvio Cycling Day) the option of a stunning circuit including both ascents of the Stelvio, a test that's never yet been set to the pros. **Information:** www.stelviopark.bz.it/it/radtag

Based on Aprica and taking place at the end of June, the **Gran Fondo La Campionissimo** ('champion of champions') was established in 2015. Thanks to some canny route planning, all three routes (85, 155 and 175 kilometres) feature the Mortirolo, although the shortest option tackles the easier side from Edolo. The two longer routes both cross the outstanding Gavia Pass and the Mazzo ascent of the Mortirolo. The longer of them goes on to the Santa Cristina. **Information:** www.granfondolacampionissimo.it/en

Other Riding

It would be almost criminal to be in Bormio and not take on the Gavia. The narrow road to the 2,621-metre pass entered cycling legend in 1988, when a snowstorm enveloped the Giro and the USA's Andy Hampsten emerged from the whiteness to claim the pink jersey, which remains his country's only success in that Grand Tour. It is entirely possible to complete a circuit from Bormio comprising the Mortirolo and Gavia via Ponte di Legno.

After looking north from Bormio to the Stelvio, east to the Gavia and south to the Mortirolo, to the west there are more Giro favourites in the shape of the Foscagno, Eira and Livigno passes. The penultimate stage of the 2010 *corsa rosa* featured all three of these 2,200-metre-plus ascents

before returning to Bormio for the passage over the Gavia and a finale on the Tonale Pass, where Swiss rider Johann Tschopp claimed by far the greatest success of his career. This gave a total distance of 178 kilometres of almost constant climbing or descending, which most would be advised to split over two days of riding.

ABOVE: The Mortirolo starts innocuously enough, the road weaving through a quiet village below the terrors hidden in the forest above.

Stage 17
Tuscany's White Roads
San Gimignano–Siena, 200km [Italy]

The Strade Bianche race stands out for a variety of reasons, most obviously for comprising more than 45 kilometres of the white gravel roads that give the event its name, but also for gaining very high status among professional riders within just a handful of years of being set up. Yet its most unlikely feature is that it turned the standard race-begets-sportive formula on its head. The professional race that was first run in 2007 and takes place in early March emerged from the highly popular Eroica Strade Bianche sportive, a *gran fondo* for vintage bikes that has taken place each October since 1997.

In 2015, the Strade Bianche started in the spectacular town of San Gimignano and finished, as it always does, in the stunning city of Siena. Although these two Tuscan beauties are set only 30 kilometres apart, this route heads south and east on sealed and unsealed roads to cover 200 kilometres. However, it can easily be shortened, as Siena is never too far away for anyone who wants to bale out early.

The rolling countryside is ideal for riders of every level. Although some of the hills are steep, they are not too long, and once roads reach the top of them they often bob along a ridge, offering wonderful views across the surrounding countryside before sweeping down into the next valley. Moreover, every few kilometres there's a tempting bakery, café or restaurant to lure you in.

Bumping gently south from San Gimignano, the route reaches the first section of white road soon after the right turn to Santa Colomba on the SP101. Swinging left towards Montalbuccio on the Strada dell'Osteriaccia, the road cuts between fields and through woodland for the next two kilometres. The limestone gravel covering the surface is small and granular and tends to be well compacted by farm traffic, resulting in a decent surface for bikes. While you need to keep an eye out for bigger stones and holes that may cause a puncture, these roads are not as relentlessly jarring as the cobbles of Flanders and Roubaix, although they can be just as dusty as the latter if big groups are riding on them.

After another two-kilometre section close to Stigliano, the third section of *sterrati*, as Italians call these unsealed roads, offers a slightly tougher test. Running south from Brucciano, this piece of white road extends to almost six kilometres and presents the first gravel climb up to Ville di

RIGHT: Punctures are an issue on the *strade bianche*, but the dusty gravel roads generally provide a good riding surface.
OPPOSITE: The wind whips the cypress trees as the pros speed down a section of white road as they race towards Siena in March's Strade Bianche.

Corsano. After a brief interlude on tarmac, the route returns to a gravelled surface, heading south from Radi towards Lupompesi and Vescovado. Running along a ridge, it looks down on vineyards and wheat fields, with cypress trees offering a typically Tuscan look to the vistas.

Another substantial section of white road from Murlo leads to Buonconvento, where there is the chance for a short cut. While the Strade Bianche route continues south to Montalcino, the finish for an epic stage in the 2010 Giro over white roads turned sludgy grey by heavy rain, a diversion east through Chiusure saves 40 kilometres. Taking this option does mean missing out on the second-longest section of *sterrati*, however, five kilometres north of Pienza.

Branching left from the SP71 next to a large cypress and signposted towards Siena (53 kilometres), it runs for more than nine kilometres,

initially along another lofty ridge before dropping down into San Giovanni d'Asso. Riding through low scrub that will remind some of outback roads in Australia and that opens out to give an expansive view across farmland, it is easy to understand how the Strade Bianche has so quickly captured the hearts of riders and fans alike. Designed and branded as 'the northern Classic that is the most southerly in Europe', it very much has the feel of Flanders and Roubaix, of exploring roads that are a throwback to a very different era, to one indeed when the bicycle was the principal mode of transport for most people.

The next sector of *sterrati* is longer still. Extending to 11.5 kilometres, this seventh section leaves the SS438 just north of Asciano. It begins with a steady climb, drops more steeply into a valley to cross a railway line, then rises steeply to Monte Sante Maria. It is a glorious stretch of road, green

ABOVE: Riders kitted out with vintage kit and bikes taking part in the Eroica sportive head along a ridge on a white road, high above the parched Tuscan countryside.

BELOW: Dust is usually the main difficulty on these gravel roads, but when it gets wet the hard-packed earth beneath the stones can turn very sludgy.

'It's the first time I've ridden it, but I love it. I think it merits consideration as a real Classic. I think it's a real pity it's not on the WorldTour calendar because if we can ride on the cobbles in WorldTour races, I think we can race on the dirt. It's a really special race.'

2015 winner Zdenek Stybar

Fact File Tuscany's White Roads

Route Details

COUNTRY: Italy
RACE: 2015 Strade Bianche
ROUTE: San Gimignano–Siena, 200km
TERRAIN: Rolling, white-gravel roads

White Roads:

SECTION 1: At km 32 for 2.2km
SECTION 2: At km 48 for 2.1km
SECTION 3: At km 55 for 5.9km
SECTION 4: At km 67 for 4.4km
SECTION 5: At km 78 for 5.5km
SECTION 6: At km 120 for 9.2km
SECTION 7: At km 146 for 11.5km
SECTION 8: At km 175 for 0.8km
SECTION 9: At km 181 for 2.4km
SECTION 10: At km 187 for 1.1km
TOTAL: 45.4km

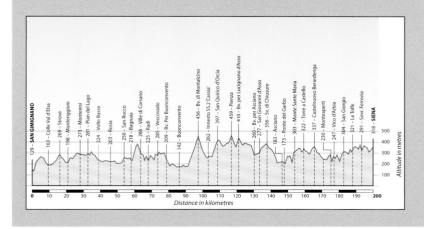

and lush in the early summer, parched and dusty later in the year. It is a disappointment to leave it for the 'proper' road to Castelnuovo Berardenga, where the route finally turns directly towards Siena.

Three short white-road sections remain, the first running from Monteaperti to Vico d'Arbia. The next up to the Colle Pinzuto begins with one of the steepest ramps of the day. Rearing up to 15 per cent, this is a critical point in the pro race, a moment to exploit a weakness in your rivals. The tenth and final *strada bianca* offers a further opportunity to do so. Again, it's not long, but a short descent leads onto a wicked climb to Le Tolfe.

Now on the northeast edge of Siena, the route circles the city anticlockwise to enter it from the southwest via the Porta di Fontebranda, where the road steepens considerably on Via Santa Caterina. It then jinks through the narrow streets and down into the shell-like Piazza del Campo, home of the Palio horse race and arguably the most dramatic location for a race finish anywhere in Europe.

OPPOSITE, TOP: The pros climb up through the narrow streets in the centre of Siena towards the Strade Bianche finish in the beautiful Piazza del Campo.
OPPOSITE, BOTTOM: Powerfully built and a superb bike-handler on rugged roads, Belgian Classics specialist Sep Vanmarcke is the kind of rider who thrives in these conditions.

Sportives

In 1997, 92 like-minded riders gathered to take part in the first edition of **L'Eroica**, a sportive designed to commemorate the history of cycle sport as well as setting the entrants a cycling challenge. That focus on history quickly became the event's guiding principle, as each year more and more riders turned out with vintage bikes and kit to ride on the white roads that would have been the terrain on which Italian racing's pioneers competed. In 2009, the organizers altered the entry qualification to permit only vintage bikes, and more than 2,500 riders took part. Four years later, such was the popularity of the event, which is based on the Tuscan town of Gaiole in Chianti, they set a ceiling of 5,000 entrants.

Registration opens in January for the early October event. There are four route options: leisure is 46 kilometres, short is 75, medium is 135 and long is 209. The two longer options cover substantial sections of the pro race that has emerged out of this very unique sportive. Those who either can't make the October date or who want to ride a contemporary bike on the course can ride any of the four routes using a roadbook that is available for a small fee through the Eroica website. It comes with a diploma that can be stamped in various partner establishments across the five regions covered by the 209-kilometre course. **Information:** www.eroicagaiole.com

Held the Sunday after the elite men and women's races and run by the same organization as the Strade Bianche, the **Gran Fondo Strade Bianche** was established in 2016. There are two routes on offer. The longer at

122 kilometres follows the same course as the professional women's race, starting and finishing in Siena and featuring 22 kilometres on the white roads. The shorter option extends to 83.5 kilometres and includes six sectors on the *strade bianche*. Both options finish in the spectacular Piazza del Campo. **Information:** www.gfstradebianche.it

Vernaccia is a renowned white-wine grape usually associated with the beautiful little town of San Gimignano, where the **Gran Fondo della Vernaccia** was based for 18 years. However, as a result of increasing demand for places, in 2016 the organizers moved the start/finish location a few kilometres east to the crystal glass-producing hill-top town of Colle Val d'Elsa. Run in early May, it offers three routes: the 165-kilometre Gran Fondo (2,100 metres of climbing), the 111-kilometre Medio Fondo (1,400 metres), and the 70-kilometre Corto Fondo (1,000 metres). There is a post-ride party in the town for all participants. Those who fancy a little bit more riding in this region might want to check out the two-day *randonnée* that the same organizers put on the previous weekend that covers 380 kilometres. **Information:** www.granfondodellavernaccia.it

Based on Florence, the **Gran Fondo Firenze** takes place in early April to the north of the city in much lumpier terrain than the events close to Siena. The Gran Fondo course is 133 kilometres long and features four substantial climbs, the highest of them the Passo del Giogo, which tops out at 882 metres. Riders are timed on the last of the climbs out of Vaglia. The 93-kilometre Medio Fondo misses the two biggest hills but does take in the Vaglia climb. **Information:** www.granfondofirenze.it/en

Other Riding

The beauty of riding in Tuscany is that it offers every type of terrain, from flat, straight roads along the Mediterranean coast to high-mountain passes in the Apennines. Thanks to this variety of riding options, its temperate climate and excellent communications, a lot of professional teams and riders base themselves here, with Lucca a particular favourite and Monte Serra, a mini-massif that sits between Lucca and Pisa, a good place to head for if you want to cross paths with or even sit on the wheel of a pro.

Further to the south, the handsome fortified hill-top town of Volterra is an ideal base from which to explore some less well-known parts of Tuscany. You'll find white roads and climbs aplenty. Among the pick of the hills is the very picturesque road up to Montecatini Val di Cecina, while there are also some lovely circuits through rolling countryside to San Gimignano. A little more to the east, it is also hard to resist the pull of the Chianti region. Located between the once-rival cities of Florence and Siena, there are roads to suit riders of every ability and plenty of gourmet options when it comes to reloading at the end of a day's riding.

RIGHT: The organizers of the Strade Bianche pro race quickly followed other events by running a sportive on the same roads used by the world's best riders.

The Twists and Turns of the Cinque Terre

Chiavari–La Spezia, 150km [Italy]

A very rugged part of the Ligurian Riviera that lies to the west of the town of La Spezia, the Cinque Terre is made up of five villages set on steep hillsides overlooking the Mediterranean. Most easily accessible by boat and train, the Cinque Terre have gained UNESCO World Heritage status because the beautiful, craggy landscape in which they sit has hardly been developed, to the extent that there are few roads. Those that do exist have interminable twists and turns that are more suited to exploration on two wheels than four.

As this protected area is not easy to access, Italy's national tour, the Giro d'Italia, has rarely ventured into the Cinque Terre. However, the race's visits to this dramatic region have become a little more frequent since the Cinque Terre, nearby Portovenere and the islands of Palmaria, Tino and Tinetto received World Heritage Status in 1997.

In 2009, the *corsa rosa*, as the Giro is known due to the *maglia rosa* ('pink jersey') that is worn by its leader, included a 60-kilometre time trial from Sestri Levante just to the north of the region, to one of the five 'lands', Riomaggiore. It was generally agreed to be one of the toughest time trials seen in a grand tour for years, which was backed up by the times posted. Winner Denis Menchov completed the course in 95 minutes, a good 20 minutes longer than usual tests of a similar length. American time-trial specialist David Zabriskie summed it up by saying, 'It was up,

down, turn, turn, turn – very technical. At the end, you're so cross-eyed, you cannot think.'

The Giro was set to return in 2012 following a storm that caused landslides that devastated the Cinque Terre the year before. However, the race's incursion had to be postponed because repairs took so long to carry out, and it wasn't until 2015 that the Giro headed back to the region. That stage covered much of the route of that 2009 time trial and many more twists and turns before the finale in La Spezia, where 22-year-old Davide Formolo announced himself as one of the home nation's big new stars with a perfectly judged victory.

Starting in Chiavari, the route initially heads southeast along the Ligurian coast to Sestri Levante, where it turns inland to Casarza Ligure and begins to climb gently up the Petronio river valley through wooded hills on the SS523. When this road continues on through a longish tunnel, cyclists should take a right turn that leads towards the day's first significant climb, the Colla di Velva, which sits on top of the hill through which the tunnel has been bored.

Dropping initially into Velva, the road climbs more steeply away from this little town to reach the summit at the Santuario di Nostra Signora della Guardia. After a lovely descent through verdant woodland, the route rejoins the SS523 at Torza and weaves its way through the trees to reach San Pietro Vara, where it turns southeast down the river valley.

Fact File The Twists and Turns of the Cinque Terre

Route Details
COUNTRY: Italy
RACE: 2015 Giro d'Italia (stage 4)
ROUTE: Chiavari–La Spezia, 150km
TERRAIN: Rolling

Climb Stats
Colla di Velva
HEIGHT: 546m
ALTITUDE GAINED: 531m
LENGTH: 14km
AVERAGE GRADIENT: 3.9%
MAXIMUM GRADIENT: 10%

Passo del Bracco
HEIGHT: 587m
ALTITUDE GAINED: 411m
LENGTH: 9km
AVERAGE GRADIENT: 4.6%
MAXIMUM GRADIENT: 7.5%

Passo del Termine
HEIGHT: 548m
ALTITUDE GAINED: 537m
LENGTH: 8.8km
AVERAGE GRADIENT: 6.4%
MAXIMUM GRADIENT: 10%

Biassa (Colle del Telegrafo)
HEIGHT: 332m
ALTITUDE GAINED: 321m
LENGTH: 4.2km
AVERAGE GRADIENT: 7.6%
MAXIMUM GRADIENT: 11%

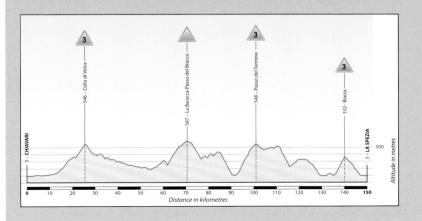

The reappearance of the *autostrada* at Brugnato brings an abrupt break from the reverie induced by this backwater road. Peace is restored, though, after Borghetto di Vara, where the road delves back into woodland. Carradano then signals the start of the second climb, the Passo del Bracco, categorized as third category for that 2009 time trial, but not at all in 2015. As this suggests, it's a steady ascent through stands of pine approaching the highest part of it on this route, which is a little short of the summit. At the La Baracca restaurant, a left turn begins the run back towards the coast and the Cinque Terre.

The descent through a pine forest offers regular glimpses of the sea, which soon fills the right-hand field of vision as the road swings left at Framura. Running parallel to the coast, the route reaches Levanto, where it climbs into the Cinque Terre National Park on the Passo del Termine. Although not fearsome, the pass does have some steeper sections, particularly after Legnano, but nothing to be very concerned about. Focus instead on the views over the rugged landscape and the sea, which are becoming increasingly impressive.

The summit comes at the junction of the SP38, rising from Levanto and continuing on to La Spezia, and the SP51, which turns off to the right and winds in breathtaking style through the Cinque Terre. Almost immediately the new road serves up a spectacular vista down into the bay that cradles the village of Monterosso al Mare, the oldest of the 'five lands', dating

ABOVE: The final climb from La Spezia up to Biassa features some of the steepest ramps on this route.
RIGHT: Wearing the pink jersey of the Giro race leader, Aussie Michael Matthews keeps tabs on his rivals sweeping through the dramatic coastal hills of the Cinque Terre.

'I think it was interesting and fun to ride. It reveals a rider's bike-handling skills. Every kind of skill can be seen on a course like this – descending and climbing, above all.'

Michael Barry

from the mid-seventh century. You barely get a chance to take it in, though, before the road is sweeping downwards through bend after bend.

On it goes, either falling or rising gently, but always twisting, offering tantalizing peeks at the shoreline 300 metres below, then tacking hard inland into dense forest. At Volastra, the trees give way to terraces that have been cut into the steep hillsides to provide farmland. Just beyond the village, the road drops away more severely, speeding past smallholdings planted with olive and fruit trees and vines.

This bottom end of the national park offers the best opportunities to visit some of the Cinque Terre. There are right turns to first Manarola and then Riomaggiore, and it's very tempting to take one of them even though the roads back up to the route are far steeper than anything else encountered on this ride. Huddled on a rocky outcrop jutting into the sea, Manarola's brightly coloured houses are wonderful, particularly when the light of the setting sun falls on them late in the day. Neighbouring Riomaggiore, which is built into a cleft in the sea cliffs, is equally dramatic.

Climbing again, the road runs parallel to the sea for the next few kilometres, giving some final views along the coast. The Cinque Terre ends when the road enters a kilometre-long tunnel. Emerging from the far end, the road weaves down into La Spezia, passing the docks, from where ferries run to the Cinque Terre.

Those determined to replicate the Giro stage have one more challenge to face, and it's well worth taking on despite initial appearances. Taking the Via Fabio Filzi out of La Spezia in almost in the same direction that you've just entered the port quickly leads to the climb up to Biassa where Formolo made good his decisive break in 2015. Once past the quarry on the early slopes, the road switches back and forth in tight and successive hairpins, more than a dozen of them all told. A left turn leads on to and over the Colle del Telegrafo. This road joins the main route into La Spezia as it emerges from the same tunnel negotiated earlier, the route then running back into the port to complete a tight and hilly finishing circuit so typical of an Italian race.

Sportives

Based on the coastal resort of Deiva Marina, mid-September's **Gran Fondo Cinque Terre** may have acted as a template for 2015's Giro stage. Its Gran Fondo (165 kilometres), Medio Fondo (87 kilometres) and Cicloturistico (61 kilometres) routes all cover much of the same ground, although they don't venture into the southerly part of the national park towards Riomaggiore and La Spezia. The longest route gains its extra distance with a very hilly loop out to the east of Borghetto di Vara, which results in a total of 3,200 metres of vertical gain. Unfortunately, the 2015 edition had to be cancelled the afternoon before it was due to take place, due to severe weather conditions. The organizers were determined to run a 20th anniversary edition in 2016. **Information:** www.granfondo5terre.com

Taking place in late May/early June in the coastal town of Massa, 20-odd kilometres south of La Spezia, the **Giro delle Alpi Apuane** ventures into the Apuan Alps of northern Tuscany, where the world-renowned Carrara marble quarries are located. The Gran Fondo (122 kilometres) and Medio Fondo (71 kilometres) both climb to more than 1,000 metres from sea level on small and relatively unknown roads that were often used by the now-retired Italian sprinter Alessandro Petacchi for training. **Information:** www.giroalpiapuane.it

The well-established **Gran Fondo Città della Spezia**, which takes place at the end of March, offers a Gran Fondo (105 kilometres) and a Medio Fondo route (80 kilometres), the longer one stacking up more than 2,000 metres of vertical gain. Traditionally, both have featured sections through the Cinque Terre, but both courses avoided the area in 2015 while resurfacing work took place on the road between the Termine pass and La Spezia in preparation for the Giro's passage. Although that temporary loss impacted on the event in terms of the spectacular, the organizers managed to find very impressive and hillier alternative roads. **Information:** www.grupposportivotarros.it

Other Riding

The undoubted pull in this area is towards the coast, but the key to enjoying the roads nearest to the Mediterranean is to venture onto them out of high season. Close to Rapallo, a beautiful resort in its own right, the village of Portofino, once renowned for its fish but now better known for its picturesque setting and celebrity visitors, is very well worth a look, even though bikes cannot be ridden or pushed through its streets. Further down the Riviera del Levante, as the coast south and east of Genoa is known, the railway runs in between the main road and the sea. However, unless you're set on following the exact route of the Giro stage that went this way, a quiet minor road running above it and through olive groves links Chiavari and Sestri Levante.

By sticking right on the coast heading south out of Sestri Levante, cyclists can avoid the traffic on the Bracco pass to reach Deiva Marina and then Framura, which is linked to Levanto via a short but unusual cycle path, running for four kilometres through a former railway tunnel. Further south, on the opposite side of the bay to La Spezia, the coastal road through Lerici (once the home of Percy Bysshe Shelley and Mary Shelley) to Montemarcello and Ameglia, is not only quiet, but is also rated by some as worthy of comparison with the Cinque Terre.

Inland, there are options at every turn. Numerous roads lead from the coast into hill-top towns and villages. Some of the most dramatic lie in the Parco Alpi Apuane just to the northeast of Sarzana, where there are some beautiful circular routes.

BELOW: The temptation to dip into each of the Cinque Terre's beautifully preserved villages is hard to resist, even though there's a tough climb out of each of them.

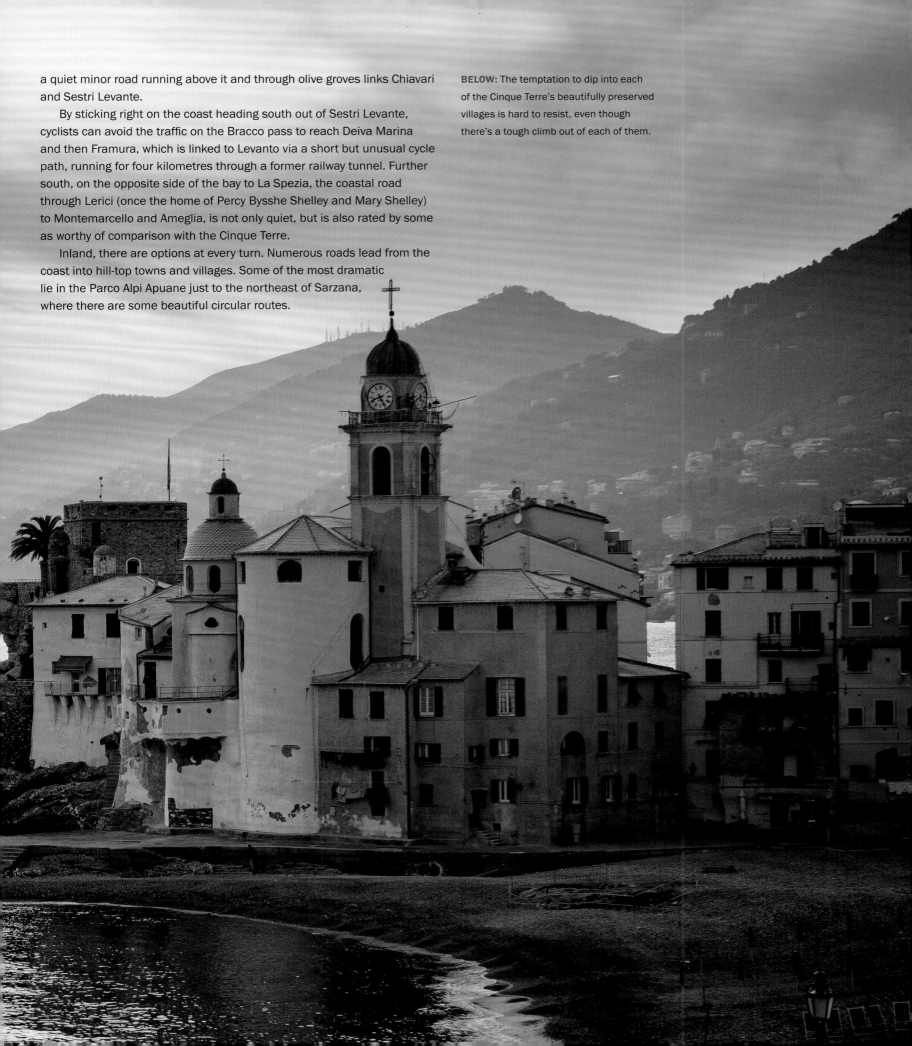

Stage ⑲
The Stage of 10,000 Corners
Ajaccio–Calvi, 145.5km [France]

When the itinerary of the 2013 Tour de France was announced, the race's then route director Jean-François Pescheux couldn't disguise his glee as he considered the third stage between Ajaccio and Calvi on the island of Corsica. 'It's the kind of stage we've been looking for for years,' Pescheux revealed, before going on to explain why. 'It's simple – there's not a single metre of flat, which means the peloton will get very stretched out, presenting the very real possibility of splits occurring, especially as, at 145 kilometres, this stage is very short.'

Pescheux and Tour director Christian Prudhomme had twin goals by starting the 2013 race on the French island. Most importantly, the three stages were the first ever to take place in Corsica as a result of long-standing concerns about possible terrorist attacks by local nationalists seeking independence from France. The fact that the Tour's management picked the 100th edition of the Tour to end this exile, thereby ensuring that the Tour had visited every one of France's domestic *départements*, only underlined its meaning.

Almost as significantly, Corsica's rugged terrain presented Pescheux and Prudhomme with an ideal opportunity to add some spice to the Tour's opening trio of stages. Running up the east side of the island, stage one was essentially flat, allowing the peloton's sprinters to lead a stampede into Bastia, headed by Germany's Marcel Kittel. Stage two crossed the island, rising to more than 1,000 metres on the Col de Vizzavona, before a complicated finish in Ajaccio that was decided by a small group of riders, led in by Belgium's Jan Bakelants. Finally, running up the northwest side of Corsica, the third stage rolled and twisted incessantly, taking in some of the island's most spectacular scenery before the finish in Calvi, where Australia's Simon Gerrans edged out Peter Sagan for victory.

This third stage started in Ajaccio, which with its airport, ferry terminal, good road connections across the island and plentiful hotels is the ideal base for two-wheeled escapades. It's rather beautiful, too.

There is almost no need to worry about getting lost on this route, either. After leaving the centre of Ajaccio on the main N194, the road passes a shopping centre on the city's outskirts and then continues for another kilometre to a roundabout, where it swings left onto the D81 which it follows for the next 140 kilometres to Calvi.

OPPOSITE: There are spectacular rides all over Corsica, but the western coast stands out partly thanks to the Tour de France's visit in 2013.

Already rising at it moves away from Ajaccio, the road climbs a little more steeply into a rocky landscape, crossing the Col de Listincone. After a brief drop, the road soon ramps up again for the bigger Col de San Bastiano, which was rated a fourth-category ascent for the Tour's stars. Over to the west, views across to the Golfe de Sagone are getting longer and more impressive with each metre of altitude gained.

Beyond the little chapel at the top of the pass, the road drops back down to sea level to loop around the lovely bay at Tiuccia. Its beauty is enhanced by the relative lack of development, a feature that the Corsican people have been fiercely determined to maintain right across the island. What development has been allowed is low-rise and as unobtrusive as possible.

BELOW: A World Heritage Site, the red sandstone outcrops of the Calanques de Piana are one of the highlights of this stage up the island's northwest coast.
OPPOSITE: There is no better way to take in this wonderful road and dramatic landscape than on a bike.

This stretch is the easiest on the route. Passing Sagone and sweeping around the upper side of the huge bay that takes its name from that little town, the road is essentially flat. It bumps up a little to reach Cargèse, its little harbour and beach tucked in behind the protective arm of a breakwater a couple of hundred feet below. North of Cargèse, the road, which has hitherto hardly been blessed with many straights, begins to wiggle even more frenetically, rising into rugged hills covered with scrubby vegetation to the San Martino pass and on into the small town of Piana.

Beyond this village lies one of the most dramatic sections of coastal road anywhere in Europe. Well above 400 metres up, it looks down into the Calanques de Piana, narrow and steep-walled inlets cut by the sea from the pinkish limestone, which turns to bright hues of red as the sun begins to set. The first hint that something extraordinary lies ahead comes a few kilometres above Piana, when the road emerges from a tight left-hander onto a 'balcony' section. A couple more turns further on, this balcony effect becomes much more pronounced when the road runs along a ledge hacked from the cliff-face. If this balustrade-less stretch twisting around bend after bend doesn't slow you down, the dramatic views will.

Weaving between crumbling pinnacles of rock, the road emerges into a much greener landscape, the hills now thickly wooded. By now it's very

LEFT AND ABOVE: While there may not be quite 10,000 corners on this route, there are plenty of them and most seem to deliver a stunning view as you round them.
PREVIOUS PAGE: As well as the stunning coast and incredible rock formations, this dramatic route also features beautifully tranquil forest roads.

clear why this was dubbed 'the stage of 10,000 corners'. One curve leads almost instantly into the next dropping into Porto, where a bakery on the far side of the viaduct over the end of the jaw-dropping Spelunca gorge provides a convenient refreshment point.

The section that follows is arguably more spectacular still, as the road climbs on a ledge high above the Gulf of Porto, headlands rippling off into the distance. Topping the Col de la Croix, which didn't even merit categorization by the Tour, the route edges inland. It leaves the sea behind for the time being, but zigs and zags no less furiously as it begins to climb another uncategorized climb, the Col de Palmarella, which marks the border between Corsica's two *départements*.

Over the next ten kilometres the road angles down gently to the scrubby Fango and Marsolino valleys, their courses mostly pebbles in the summer months after the high-mountain snows have melted. The route follows the Marsolino for half a dozen kilometres before starting up the pass of the same name. This col is quite different to the earlier ones, the road sweeping up in broad curves above the wide valley, then dropping down the far side in the same fashion.

Running into Calvi, the road runs with hardly a deviation until it's past the tiny airport. Rather than continue into the port, it turns right onto the N197, then again onto the D151, to finish on the other side of the runway on a dusty and very nondescript road. It is next to the headquarters of the French Foreign Legion's 2nd Parachute Regiment, which was clearly chosen to accommodate the Tour's immense convoy of vehicles and other paraphernalia.

However, without that massive logistical concern to worry about, a better alternative is to continue directly into Calvi, where the citadel jutting proudly into the sea offers a finale more fitting with the spectacle laid on before.

ABOVE: This view through the Calanques de Piana reveals the engineering work undertaken both above and below the road to ensure its passage.

Sportives

Centred on Bastia, the two-day **Cyclo'Corse** covers territory that the Tour de France did not venture into during its three-day stay in 2013, principally the Cap de Corse peninsula that juts up like a thumb from the northeastern tip of the island. Taking place in mid-April, the two days are quite different. The first covers 70 kilometres and includes two timed sections on the Col de la Vierge and the Col de Teghime. The second day is a more traditional sportive, its two route options covering 100 and 130 kilometres respectively. **Information:** www.challengecyclotour.com/cyclocorse.htm

Less a sportive and more of a tour, the **Cent Cols Challenges** are organized by elite-end cycle clothing manufacturer Rapha and take place in northern Spain, the Pyrenees, the Alps, the Dolomites and, in this case, Corsica. Extending to 11 days and covering every corner of Corsica, the stages vary between 160 and 220 kilometres in length. As the '100 Passes' name suggests, there is a lot of climbing involved, an average of no less than 3,800 metres per day. However, the burden is eased by

Route Details
COUNTRY: France
RACE: 2013 Tour de France (stage 3)
ROUTE: Ajaccio–Calvi, 145.5km
TERRAIN: Rolling

Climb Stats
Col de San Bastiano
HEIGHT: 411m
ALTITUDE GAINED: 158m
LENGTH: 3km
AVERAGE GRADIENT: 5.3%
MAXIMUM GRADIENT: 6.8%

Col de San Martino
HEIGHT: 430m
ALTITUDE GAINED: 410m
LENGTH: 7.7km
AVERAGE GRADIENT: 5.3%
MAXIMUM GRADIENT: 8.3%

Côte de Porto
HEIGHT: 161m
ALTITUDE GAINED: 128m
LENGTH: 2km
AVERAGE GRADIENT: 6.4%
MAXIMUM GRADIENT: 8%

Col de Marsolino
HEIGHT: 443m
ALTITUDE GAINED: 267m
LENGTH: 3.3km
AVERAGE GRADIENT: 8.1%
MAXIMUM GRADIENT: 9.2%

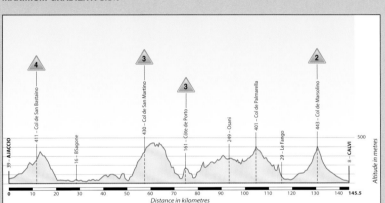

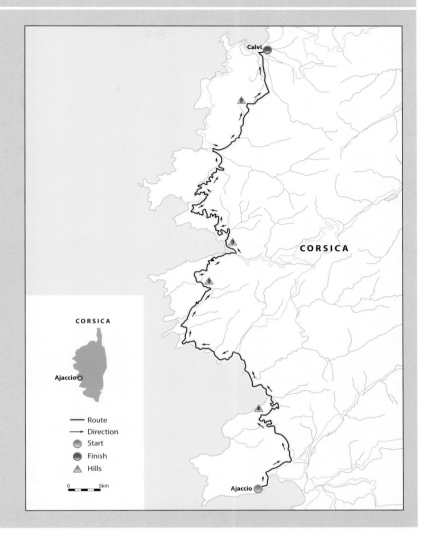

the organizers transferring each rider's luggage to the end-of-ride hotel each day and by the relative ease of the climbs on the French island. **Information:** www.centcolschallenge.com/routes/corsica

The locally run **Tour de Corse** also takes place over 11 days, but those days are not as long, nor as hilly. The stages cover between 85 and 120 kilometres, with between 1,000 and 2,300 metres of climbing. The tour takes place three times a year – the first in late April, the second in early September and the third at the end of that month – and, like the Cent Cols, covers much of the island. **Information:** www.corsecyclotourisme.org/tour_corse.html

Other Riding
The beauty of Corsica for cyclists is that there are many, many great rides all over the island, most of them little used even in the height of the tourist season. The Corsica Cyclist website (www.corsicacyclist.com) is a mine of information about rides all over the island, including all three stages from the 2013 Tour and other pro races that have taken place in Corsica,

including late March's Critérium International, which has been staged here since 2010. Comprising a long road stage on the Saturday, then a short time trial and a short mountain stage on the Sunday, it has usually been decided atop the Col de l'Ospedale, in southern Corsica. It can be tackled via an 83-kilometre loop from the lovely little town of Porto Vecchio, the incongruous location of the 2013 Tour's Grand Départ. Running up to this pass through thick pine forest, the loop continues over the Illarta, Pelza and Bacino passes on the way back to Porto Vecchio.

Among the best options in the centre of the island is the beautiful run on the minor D84. It goes from the village of Francardo through gorges and forests and over a number of passes, including Corsica's highest, to Porto and then through the *calanques* (inlets) to Piana. It's spectacular from the off, the road cut from granite cliffs before the long climb up to the 1,480-metre Col de Vergio. The road descends through thick pine forest to Évisa, beyond which, if anything, it gets even more dramatic as it runs parallel to the Gorges de Spelunca. A haven of glassy pools protected by towering cliffs and rocky outcrops, it is well worthy of comparison with the UNESCO World Heritage ride to Piana.

BELOW: The Calanques de Piana – once ridden, never forgotten.

Côte d'Azur Rock 'n' Roll

Brignoles–Cannes, 200km [France]

Universally known as 'the race to the sun', Paris–Nice signals the arrival of spring in the European cycling season. Traditionally, this very prestigious race, which runs over eight days in the second week of March, begins in or very close to the French capital, which is often still cloaked by winter mist and chill. Over the following few days, the race takes giant southward leaps to reach the Midi, where the peloton spends three days in the sun, the sudden warmth adding vigour to the battle for the leader's white jersey, which is ultimately decided in the hills inland from the Côte d'Azur.

Most of the hills behind Provence's Mediterranean coast don't amount to much of a test taken in isolation. However, stringing as many as nine or ten of them together,

ABOVE: Alberto Contador goes on the attack climbing the Col du Tanneron in 2007's Paris–Nice.

RIGHT AND OPPOSITE: The route offers a good mix of recognizably French terrain, from plane-bordered roads to tunnels carved through rock.

PREVIOUS PAGE: You can almost smell the scent of pine as the pro bunch sweeps through a corner heading for Cannes.

as Paris–Nice's organizers ASO tend to do on the penultimate day of the event, will undoubtedly result in a significant shake-out within the peloton, and this stage is a perfect example of that.

It comes from the 2007 edition of 'the race to the sun', which heralded the arrival of Alberto Contador as the dominant stage-race rider of the era. Running from Brignoles, which lies 50 kilometres inland in the heart of the Var, to glitzy Cannes, so often the finishing point for this hilly stage, it crosses no fewer than nine passes. Just one of them is more than six kilometres in length, but they come almost relentlessly, especially in the latter half of the stage, and conclude with one of this race's iconic ascents, the Col du Tanneron, which sits right behind Cannes.

Although Cannes lies due east of Brignoles, the route heads off to the north through Le Val and towards the first of the nine climbs, the Côte de Réal Martin, rated third category in 2007 and little more than 1,500 metres in length. The road is typical of Provence, with gravel chippings coating the tar underlayer. It makes for a grippy surface, which the pros describe as 'heavy', as wheels don't roll as easily as they do on smooth tarmac. The other drawback is that the surface can become slippery on hot days, when the tar liquefies a touch and can yield, particularly and most dangerously when cornering. That shouldn't be an issue this early in the ride, though, as the road eases upwards past vineyards and stands of pine.

Beyond Barjols the road climbs steadily again to Tavernes where, rather than continuing north towards the awe-inspiring Verdon Gorge, a thrilling diversion on another day, the route turns eastwards for the first time. Still rising through woods of oak, eucalyptus and chestnut, the road passes the curiously named hill-top village of Fox-Amphoux and winds quietly on to

Sillans-la-Cascade, a lovely oasis of shade with a waterfall that's hard to resist on days beset by *la canicule*, the oppressive heat that affects the Midi in the summer months.

After rounding the ceramics centre of Salernes, the road gets a little busier – and better surfaced! – as it arrows towards Lorgues, passing rickety fruit stands selling melons and luscious Provençal peaches. The road dips into Taradeau, with its medieval tower, then climbs away from it on the second notable climb of the day, which signals the start of a much more undulating passage. The climb out of Taradeau is one of the steeper hills, but it's only two kilometres long, so not excessive. It is, though, the constant run of short hills like this that will gradually take a toll.

Next up, soon after the military centre of Draguignan, is a Paris–Nice favourite, the Côte de Tuillières, another short ascent but with the highest average all day. Cresting it, there's a fabulous view across the hills rippling away into the heat haze, but there's barely time to take it in before sweeping down to a junction and a left turn that soon leads on to another Paris–Nice regular, the Col de St-Andrieux.

Now, in what has long been one of the key battlegrounds in 'the race to the sun', there's hardly more than a few hundred metres between hills. Dropping out of St-Andrieux and passing the village of Montferrat, the road quickly rises once again towards the Col du Défens. At the summit, the route takes a right onto the smaller D19 and trundles downhill and onto a plateau, which offers brief respite from the Var rollercoaster.

This restorative interlude ends as the road winds around the lower part of the impressive hill-top village of Bargemon. The undulations return, but the magnificence of the terrain and the road weaving through pine forest distracts

from the increase in effort, the trees on the roadsides frequently coming together to create a canopy that provides a very welcome respite from the sun.

Approaching the medieval hill-top village of Seillans, renowned as one of the prettiest in France, the forest where oak, cork, hornbeam and pine predominate thickens. A steady loss in altitude continues beyond Seillans, the road a little busier as it heads for Fayence, another of the south-facing hill-top villages in this area that are a huge draw for tourists from the Côte d'Azur.

Rather than staying on the eastward path towards Cannes, the route turns to the north towards the longest climb of the day, the ten-kilometre-long Col de Bourigaille. Also known as the Col d'Avaye, it begins among olive groves as the road moves away from Fayence and wends its way up woods filled with several types of oak. The gradient rarely approaches double figures, but on a sizzling day with 130 kilometres already covered, it will seem steeper than that to many riders.

Cresting it, the road drops only briefly before climbing again on the penultimate hill, the Côte de Mons, which has been cut out of the rockface over a deep ravine, making for some dramatic views. Tightly packed on an outcrop at the top of the pass, Mons is arguably the most spectacular of the hill-top villages in the Pays de Fayence, based on vistas that extend as far as Corsica on a very clear day.

From this, the highest point of the day, the road tumbles down through the woods for some distance, climbs briefly again, then rushes down towards Callian, forking left to neighbouring Montauroux, zipping across the main road to Grasse and heading towards Tanneron, where the last hill awaits. The lower reaches of the Col du Tanneron, almost an essential on the Paris–Nice route, very much resemble the backcountry climbs earlier on, and it's hard to believe that Cannes is only a dozen kilometres away. That thought will immediately disappear, though, as you hit the section at 18 per cent that continues for a few hundred metres.

Higher up the road is bordered by villas with azure pools and the oaks give way to manicured cypress. The perfume centre of Grasse emerges over to the left. Then, having negotiated the tight hairpins on the descent off the Tanneron, the route enters Pégomas and the edge of the finishing city. A quick blast down the D9 leads into the buzzing centre of Cannes and soon after to the glamorous Boulevard de la Croisette, home to the world-famous film festival. It could hardly be less in keeping with what has gone before, but what a setting it is to cool off.

Sportives

The opening event on the Grand Trophée calendar, which also includes the Trois Ballons in the Vosges and La Vaujany near Alpe d'Huez, early April's **Gran Fondo Gassin Golfe de Saint-Tropez** starts and finishes in the exclusive Mediterranean resort. There are three route options, each of them looping out into the rugged Massif des Maures, where the roads are very similar to those around Brignoles, Draguignan and Seillans. There are lots of hills, the highest of them the 680-metre Notre Dame des Anges, and almost constant undulations. As a result, the 160-kilometre Gran Fondo route clocks up more than 2,600 metres of vertical gain, while the 132-kilometre Medio Fondo is only a couple of hundred metres behind that total. The 77-kilometre Rando has half that amount. **Information:** www.grandtrophee.fr/epreuve.php?C=4

Fact File Côte d'Azur Rock 'n' Roll

Route Details

COUNTRY: France
RACE: 2007 Paris–Nice (stage 6)
ROUTE: Brignoles–Cannes, 200km
TERRAIN: Medium mountain

Climb Stats

Côte de Réal Martin
HEIGHT: 301m
ALTITUDE GAINED: 99m
LENGTH: 1.7km
AVERAGE GRADIENT: 5.8%
MAXIMUM GRADIENT: 7%

Côte de Taradeau
HEIGHT: 235m
ALTITUDE GAINED: 144m
LENGTH: 2km
AVERAGE GRADIENT: 7.2%
MAXIMUM GRADIENT: 9%

Côte des Tuillières
HEIGHT: 390m
ALTITUDE GAINED: 180m
LENGTH: 2.3km
AVERAGE GRADIENT: 7.8%
MAXIMUM GRADIENT: 20%

Col de St-Andrieux
HEIGHT: 504m
ALTITUDE GAINED: 219m
LENGTH: 4.3km
AVERAGE GRADIENT: 5.1%
MAXIMUM GRADIENT: 8%

Col du Défens
HEIGHT: 648m
ALTITUDE GAINED: 191m
LENGTH: 3.9km
AVERAGE GRADIENT: 4.9%
MAXIMUM GRADIENT: 8%

Col de Bourigaille
HEIGHT: 780m
ALTITUDE GAINED: 525m
LENGTH: 10.3km
AVERAGE GRADIENT: 5.1%
MAXIMUM GRADIENT: 11%

Côte de Mons
HEIGHT: 802m
ALTITUDE GAINED: 126m
LENGTH: 1.8km
AVERAGE GRADIENT: 7%
MAXIMUM GRADIENT: 11%

Col du Tanneron
HEIGHT: 372m
ALTITUDE GAINED: 307m
LENGTH: 5.8km
AVERAGE GRADIENT: 5.3%
MAXIMUM GRADIENT: 18%

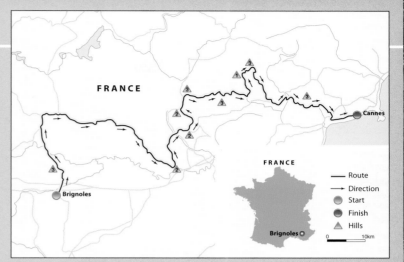

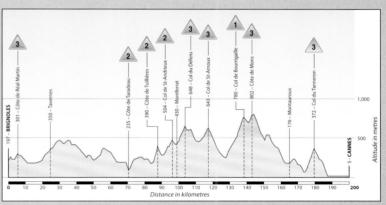

BELOW: Inland from the mildness of the Côte d'Azur, spring has yet to fully bloom in this rugged terrain.

There's good reason why late May's **Boucles du Verdon** avoids the most jaw-dropping sections of the Verdon Gorge. The most spectacular part of it, just before the Verdon feeds into the turquoise waters of Lac de Ste-Croix, have such a pull on the eye that sending hundreds of cyclists along it would be asking for trouble. Despite this omission, the two routes based on St André les Alpes will impress. Both the 150-kilometre Grande route (2,500 metres of vertical gain) and the 83-kilometre Petite option (1,200 metres of vertical gain) include climbs that have featured in Paris–Nice, their courses venturing into the southern edge of the Alps. Don't miss the Grand Canyon du Verdon if you do head this way, as it's one of Europe's great natural wonders. In fact, why not indulge in a full-on Verdon experience by warming up with a ride along the gorge on the Saturday followed by the sportive on the Sunday? **Information:** www.bouclesduverdon.fr

A number of smaller sportives cover the roads that regularly feature in Paris–Nice, including two that pay tribute to great names of French cycling. Late April's **La Louis Caput**, organized by the Villeneuve-Loubet cycling club, pays tribute to the 1946 French national champion and former team director with two routes (100 and 150 kilometres) that both set out over the Col de Vence, long associated with 'the race to the sun'. The following weekend's **La Lazaridès** honours the memory of Apo Lazaridès, twice a top-ten finisher at the Tour de France and president of the ES Cannes club that organizes the event. The Col de l'Estérel, Col de Bourigaille, Côte de Mons and the Tanneron all feature on the longer of the two routes. Starting and finishing in Vence and organized by the club in that town, May's **La Vençoise** climbs both sides of the Col de Vence, the longer 150-kilometre route (the shorter option is 105 kilometres) extending as far west as St-Auban and the nearby Col de Bleine, which tops out at 1,439 metres. **Information:** www.esvlcyclo.fr (La Louis Caput)
www.etoilesportivedecannes.fr (La Lazaridès)
www.ccvence.fr (La Vençoise)

Other Riding

Any exploration of the Provençal battlegrounds of 'the race to the sun' should be extended to the east to include the mountainous roads immediately to the north of Nice and Monaco. The first stop should be the Col d'Èze, which climbs from the eastern end of Nice and is part of one of the Corniche roads that run between the city and Monaco. Although little more than 500 metres in height, the Col d'Èze has regularly been the decisive point in the race, particularly when tackled in a time trial. Many professional riders live in this area, including Chris Froome, Richie Porte and Philippe Gilbert. Their training runs take them into the bigger hills further inland, among which the most renowned is the Col de la Madone, near Gorbio. It was Lance Armstrong's preferred climb when testing his form, and gave its name to Trek's top-of-the-range road bike. The Madone is not to be confused with the Col de la Madone d'Utelle, a stage finish in the 2016 edition of Paris–Nice, which lies due north of Nice. When pros based in this region are preparing for the grand tours, they will often head out to the Col de Turini at the bottom end of the Mercantour National Park.

RIGHT: The Paris–Nice peloton passes under a Provençal town hall as the 2007 stage heads for Cannes.

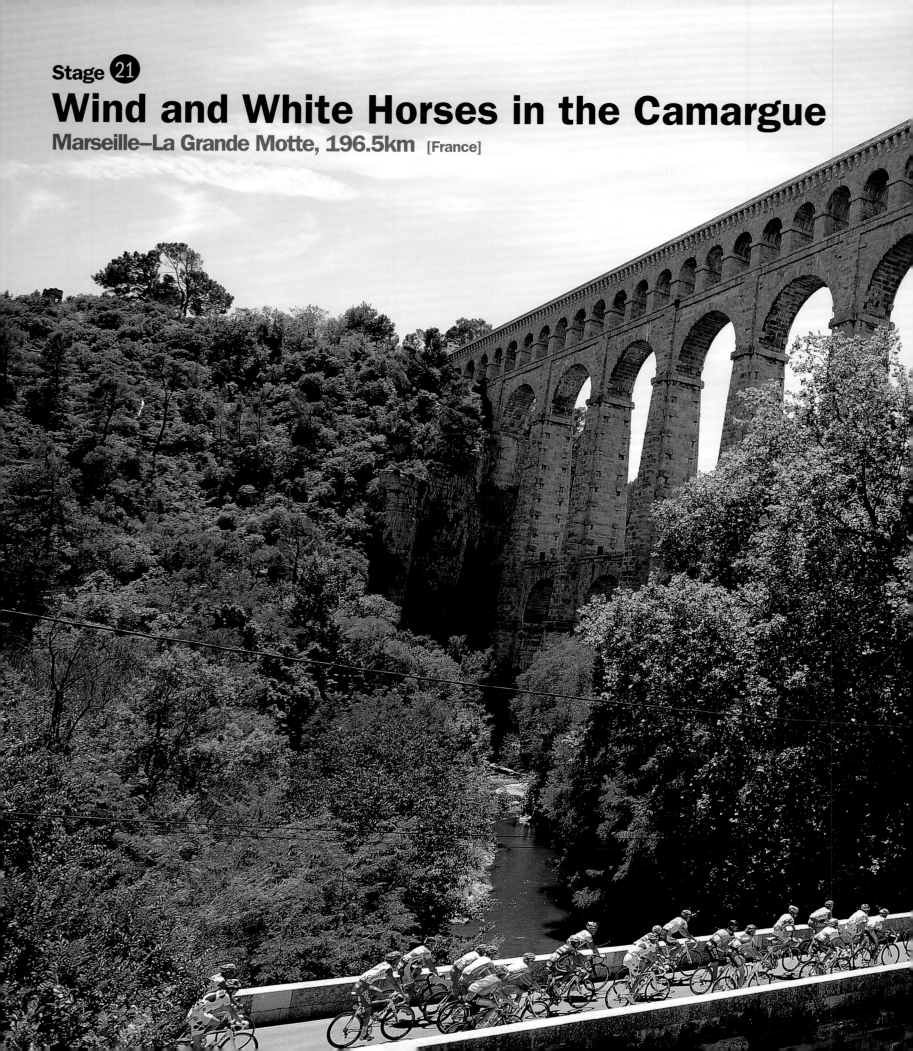

Wind and White Horses in the Camargue

Marseille–La Grande Motte, 196.5km [France]

While France's Mediterranean coast may have a well-deserved reputation as a haven for sun-seekers, the Bouches du Rhône region to the west of Marseille offers something very different to the sandy beaches and pine-scented hills that stick in the memory of most visitors to this area. The Camargue National Park features Europe's largest river delta, its unspoiled expanse of marshes, lagoons and waterways extending to almost 1,000 square kilometres that are home to a huge variety of flora and fauna, including its famous flamingos and white horses. To the east of this watery wilderness, where hardly any development has taken place, lies the similarly untouched Crau region, a mixture of arid and marshy pastureland.

With few towns and little-used roads, the Camargue and the Crau are ideal for exploration by bike, as long as you're prepared for a bit of buffeting from the wind. In summer, the wind is generally onshore, blowing in off the Med. However, the mistral, which comes from the north, can also become a factor. Although this persistent and often very strong wind tends to barrel down the Rhône valley and out into the Mediterranean during winter and spring, it can blow just as urgently during the summer, clearing the air and restoring the Côte d'Azur's cloudless aspect as it does so.

The Tour de France first ventured into this region during its inaugural edition, in 1903, when the riders set off from Marseille late on in a very hot evening and raced across the Crau to Arles with the mistral harrying

them all the way. More than a century later, the 2009 race traversed the Crau and Camargue on another wind-affected stage out of Marseille. With around 30 kilometres to the finish, the route turned side on to the mistral, making it likely that echelons would form if any team chose to increase the speed at this critical moment. Mark Cavendish's HTC-Columbia team opted to do exactly that, their injection of pace splitting the peloton into several sections and eventually leaving the Manxman with a far more straightforward sprint to the stage victory in La Grande Motte than he would otherwise have had.

That stage started in Marseille's Vieux Port, a very glamorous setting that helps dispel the much-revitalized port city's former reputation for criminality and danger. Rolling away from the impressive marina, the route winds through Marseille to reach L'Estaque on the eastern edge of the city. Passing the beach and the marina, it follows the coast initially before turning inland through low hills of white rock to Le Rove and Gignac-la-Nerthe, close to the Marignane airport that serves Marseille.

The next few kilometres through the messy industrial hinterland to the north of Marseille are not memorable, although the landscape is a lot more inviting once the road zigs in and out of Les Pennes-Mirabeau. Rising away from the bustle of Marseille's outskirts, the road passes through the lower tier of arches of the dramatic Roquefavour aqueduct, a 19th-century creation modelled on the renowned Pont du Gard, a Roman equivalent close to Nîmes.

'The Camargue is a region where there's not the slightest bit of shelter from the wind.'

Jean-François Pescheux,
ex-Tour de France route director

If the mistral is gusting, this section will be almost into the teeth of it, but the upside of that is that the wind should provide a good deal of assistance later in the day, which is well worth remembering as the route soon switches to the northwest and a head-on encounter with the sapping breeze.

Tracking the course of the River Arc as it takes a broad sweep around the Étang de Berre lagoon, the road gets busier as it passes close to the junction of the A7 and A8 autoroutes, but quietens off again beyond Les Guigues, where verdant vineyards stretch away across the landscape towards the low ridge that harbours the first of two categorized climbs. The Côte de Calissanne merited only fourth-category status in 2009 and doesn't go much above 100 metres in height, but so flat is the terrain to the south and west that the views from it are extensive.

Undulating gently, the road continues past a military firing range towards Salon-de-Provence, only to cut away from this historical city – where the seer Nostradamus lived and is buried – to reach Grans and the fertile flatlands on the eastern edge of the Crau. Tacking due north again into very open countryside where the trees all lean quite noticeably in the other direction, the road makes a beeline towards Eyguières, gateway to the Alpilles Regional Park.

An extension of the Luberon range to the east, the Alpilles massif runs for 25 kilometres between the Rhône and Durance rivers. The highest point is the 498-metre Tour des Opies, lying just north of the road as it moves in a westerly direction away from Eyguières. While far from alpine in stature, this range of hills stands out quite surprisingly because its weathered limestone outcrops rise up so abruptly from the pan-flat Crau plain. They take a little of the edge off the mistral when it is blowing, as does the *maquis*, the generic name for the low scrub that covers most of this stony ground.

Running almost dead straight along the northern edge of the Crau, the route reaches Maussane-les-Alpilles, where it starts to climb once again. It rises through woodland initially, then breaks out into more open country to reach the highest point of the ride, the 186-metre-high Col de la Vayède, just before Les Baux-de-Provence, one of France's most beautiful villages, which sits on an outcrop beneath a crumbling ruin of a castle. Located at around halfway, this is an ideal place for lunch, especially as onward progress begins with a gentle descent back down through olive and almond groves to the plain.

ABOVE: The magnificent town of Les Baux-de-Provence, which sits atop an outcrop in the Alpilles range.
PREVIOUS PAGE: Modelled on the Roman Pont du Gard, the 19th-century Roquefavour aqueduct, which lies just north of Marseille, is just one of many architectural highlights along this route.

Soon after passing the quite startling fortified Montmajour Abbey, a frequent subject for Vincent Van Gogh, the route enters the beautiful Roman city of Arles, the largest municipality in France thanks to the inclusion of a large part of the Camargue, which lies to the south and west. Immediately after crossing the Rhône, the route turns south to run alongside the Grand-Rhône, as the bigger part of the river is now known after its course split just north of Arles.

Even though a high embankment conceals the river, this is a lovely stretch, particularly if the wind is favourable. After a few kilometres, the route turns away from the river and towards the Camargue wetlands, where farmland soon gives way to thickets of marshland and rushes, which form high hedges that billow frantically in the wind. It reaches Étang de Vaccarès, a vast saltwater lagoon that's no more than two metres deep and is home to hundreds of different breeds of migratory birds, including flamingos.

At Albaron, the road meets the Petit-Rhône and follows the river as it meanders towards the sea. After ten kilometres, the route reaches the point where the 2009 Tour stage was blown apart, a right turn sending the course almost back on itself. It might seem a little odd that such an innocuous-looking piece of road could leave the world's best racers struggling to hang on to their rivals. However, when the peloton lines out due to a change in the wind direction and an increase in pace, even the tiniest gap that opens up between riders quickly becomes unbridgeable.

The white horses are most likely to appear in the marshy stretch either side of the bridge over the Petit-Rhône. There are also signs for Camargue rice, underlining to what extent water dominates this region.

At Aigues-Mortes, the route switches onto the dual carriageway that blasts along the final section towards La Grande Motte along the northern side of the Étang du Ponant. This suited the Tour riders lining up for a bunch sprint, but the better option for riders who want to finish with something less frenetic is to stay on the smaller road to Le Grau-du-Roi and enter the popular beach resort of La Grande Motte from the east rather than the north. It means that the ride concludes in the same alluring way it started, by rolling alongside the Med.

Sportives

Organized by VC La Pomme, the Marseille club for which Dan Martin, Nicolas Roche and many others rode before stepping up into the pro ranks, late September's **Bosses du 13** (also known as the **Les Bosses du Provence**) is a two-day event. It offers two short *randonnées* routes on the Saturday and a choice of three cyclosportive routes on the Sunday. All of the routes feature the Col de la Gineste, a staple route for Marseille riders and the final climb in the season-opening GP de la Marseillaise, the randos then heading to the coast around Cassis and La Ciotat before returning to the port city. The sportives tackle a number of climbs that are well used in pro events, notably the Gineste, the Col de l'Ange and the Col de l'Espigoulier. The longest option is 164 kilometres (2,442 metres of vertical gain) and tackles both sides of those three ascents. The two shorter options are 136 kilometres (2,037 metres) and 94 kilometres (1,426 metres). There are also events for children on a closed kilometre-long circuit. **Information:** www.bossesdu13.fr

La Royale Camarguaise is an ideal way to see the unique Camargue wetlands and get the legs going at the start of the sportive season. Based on the town of Lunel, just to the east of Montpellier, and run in early March, the event offers four routes, the shortest extending to 60 kilometres and the longest to 150 and covering just about the whole extent of the national park. With a total of only 350 metres of vertical gain for the 150-kilometre option, this event doesn't sound too taxing, but beware of the mistral as it can be fierce at this time of year.
Information: pth.sudvelo.com/protour/la-royale-camarguaise

One climb dominates this part of France: the legendary Tour de France ascent of Mont Ventoux. Little more than 100 kilometres north of Marseille, 'The Giant of Provence' features in a number of sportives, of which two of the best renowned are the **Gran Fondo Mont Ventoux Beaumes-de-Venise** and **GFNY Mont Ventoux**. The former, part of the Grand Trophée series, takes place in early June. Based on the celebrated winemaking centre of Beaumes-de-Venise, it offers three routes, each of them featuring at least one ascent to the Ventoux's summit. The latter takes place in late June and features two routes based on Vaison-la-Romaine and finishing atop the Ventoux. Those who can't get enough of the Ventoux might want to consider a bid to enter the **Club des Cinglés du Mont Ventoux**, which translates loosely as the brotherhood of Mont Ventoux obsessives. To gain admission riders must climb all three sides of the mountain within 24 hours on any day of their choice, getting the club's validatation form stamped along the way.
Information: www.grandtrophee.fr/epreuve.php?C=121
www.gfnymontventoux.com
www.clubcinglesventoux.org

Other Riding

The main difficulty in this heavily populated and very busy part of the Midi is finding quiet roads to ride on. To the west of Marseille, the roads on the southern side of the Chaîne de l'Estaque fit the bill, while to the east the most regular choice for riders in Marseille's VC La Pomme is the Massif de la Sainte-Baume beyond the town of Gémenos. There aren't many roads in the Camargue, but it is possible to get away from traffic of almost any kind by following the back roads that run parallel to the Grand-Rhône as it flows south from Arles towards Port-St-Louis-du-Rhône. To the north of Montpellier, the Cévennes National Park is criss-crossed by tiny and seldom-used roads. The most renowned climb in this massif is lofty Mont Aigoual, which can be reached by a number of stunning roads.

OPPOSITE: All of the climbing comes in the first half of this route, principally in the Alpilles.
PREVIOUS PAGE: Large parts of the Camargue have been drained to create fertile farmland.

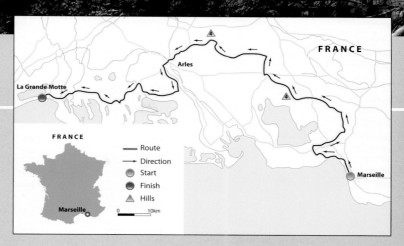

Fact File Wind and White Horses in the Camargue

Route Details

COUNTRY: France

RACE: 2009 Tour de France (stage 3)

ROUTE: Marseille–La Grande Motte, 196.5km

TERRAIN: Small hills but mostly flat

Climb Stats

Côte de Calissanne

HEIGHT: 126m

ALTITUDE GAINED: 107m

LENGTH: 1.3km

AVERAGE GRADIENT: 5.5%

MAXIMUM GRADIENT: 8%

Col de la Vayède

HEIGHT: 183m

ALTITUDE GAINED: 52m

LENGTH: 0.7km

AVERAGE GRADIENT: 7.4%

MAXIMUM GRADIENT: 10%

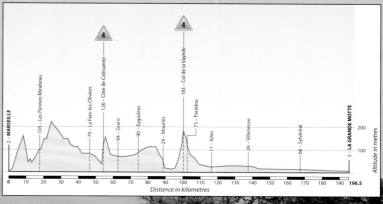

Stage (22)
The Pyrenean Alpe d'Huez
Mazamet–Plateau de Beille, 197km [France]

The Pyrenees may not offer challenges as lofty as those in the Alps, but the climbs in this massif can be just as testing as those in the Tour de France's other principal mountain playground. This stage from the 2007 Tour exemplifies this perfectly.

Bar one shortish ascent near the start in Mazamet, the main centre in the rugged Montagne Noire that looks across the Corbières and Minervois vineyards to the Pyrenees, the climbing is all in the back end of the stage. Yet the pass of the Port de Pailhères and the zig-zagging climb up to the Plateau de Beille ski station are well capable of derailing even the ablest mountain goats. In typical Pyrenean fashion, the Pailhères'

gradient changes regularly, making it difficult to maintain a rhythm, while Plateau de Beille has, like Luz Ardiden, been described as 'the Pyrenean Alpe d'Huez' as its road switchbacks steeply up to almost 1,800 metres, averaging eight per cent for 16 kilometres.

These two mighty ascents are hidden in the haze as this ride begins in Mazamet, home to former French favourite Laurent Jalabert and also to Christophe Bassons, one of the very few riders who raced cleanly around the millennium and stood up for the principle of doing so. Both cut their teeth on the wickedly undulating roads of the Montagne Noire, although the initial test of the Côte de Saraille, which merited second-category

BELOW: A summer storm sweeps across the upper part of the climb to Plateau de Beille.

ABOVE: When the snows melt and the Tour de France isn't in the area, this ski station becomes the domain of livestock and hill walkers.

status in the 2007 Tour, is not all that typical of the climbs in this heavily forested area. It is tree-lined and attractive, but nothing like as exacting as the nearby Pic de Nore.

Crossing the watershed, this main road from Mazamet to Carcassonne swings down gently towards the plain that sits between the Montagne Noire and the Pyrenees. As the gradient eases, the road straightens, speeding towards the main city in the Aude, the first encounter with the Canal du Midi a signal that Carcassonne and its magnificent walled citadel are just minutes away.

Having started on the D118 in Mazamet, the route follows this road as it heads through Carcassonne and continues south towards the ever-clearer, jagged line of the Pyrenees. Passing vineyards and occasionally kissing the banks of the River Aude, the road makes a beeline for the mountains, its directness finally halted by bustling Limoux, home to *blanquette*, the sparkling white wine that inspired winegrowers in Champagne and remains very much the fizz of choice in this corner of France.

Entering the upper Aude valley south of Limoux, the road weaves with the river as wooded hills squeeze in on both sides. Beyond Quillan, where the D117 temporarily replaces the D118 as the southerly route, signs for rafting expeditions hint at a change in the gradient, which becomes more pronounced on the return to the D118 as the road turns towards Axat. Soon after, the road and river cut through the tight Saint-Georges Gorge, which is effectively a gateway between the easy going to this point and the much more complicated terrain that now lies ahead.

Hydroelectric plants appear almost as regularly as oncoming vehicles. The steepling and heavily forested hillsides suggest that some serious climbing is not too far away, but conceal the mountains from view as the road snakes up the Aude Gorge to Usson-les-Bains, where the route forks right towards the ski station at Mijanès. This is where the Port de Pailhères starts, and initially the going is easy. However, the sudden appearance of the crumbling Château d'Usson, a 12th-century Cathar stronghold, heralds a change.

At the junction of the D16 and D216, there's a choice. Both climb to Rouze, the former gaining height through a string of hairpins, the latter continuing more directly and steeply. The professionals were given the first option in 2007. Between Rouze and Mijanès, the gradient is not too fierce and the views are fabulous. Once past Mijanès, though, there are some more abrupt ramps on what is now a narrow ribbon of road.

Passing the cluster of buildings that make up the Mijanès ski station, the toughest part of the climb begins. Running up the side of a valley with beautiful woodland, the gradient is close to ten per cent and there are long views ahead to the top of the pass. But a sudden flurry of hairpins distracts from this thought. Soon after, there's another flurry, which carry the road above the trees and into an immense natural amphitheatre, an arena that undoubtedly offers one of the best spectating points anywhere in the cycling world. By the time the road emerges from the next gaggle of switchbacks, the experience is completely breathtaking and you're left wondering how this amazing pass has remained relatively unknown.

The pass tops out at one metre above 2,000, then plummets towards Ax-les-Thermes. The first half-dozen kilometres are steep and fast. It is easy to understand why, in the 2013 Tour, French hope Thibaut Pinot lost

Fact File The Pyrenean Alpe d'Huez

Route Details

COUNTRY: France
RACE: 2007 Tour de France (stage 14)
ROUTE: Mazamet–Plateau de Beille, 197km
TERRAIN: High mountains

Climb Stats

Côte de Saraille

HEIGHT: 810m
ALTITUDE GAINED: 468m
LENGTH: 9km
AVERAGE GRADIENT: 5.2%
MAXIMUM GRADIENT: 8%

Port de Pailhères

HEIGHT: 2,001m
ALTITUDE GAINED: 1,207m
LENGTH: 14.9km
AVERAGE GRADIENT: 8.1%
MAXIMUM GRADIENT: 12%

Plateau de Beille

HEIGHT: 1,790m
ALTITUDE GAINED: 1,255m
LENGTH: 15.8km
AVERAGE GRADIENT: 7.9%
MAXIMUM GRADIENT: 11%

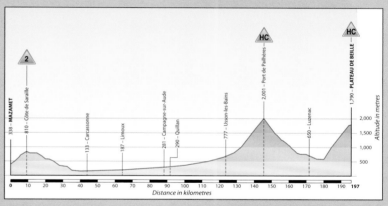

LEFT: The Tour peloton lines out to negotiate a narrow Pyrenean descent.

NEXT PAGE: The weather in the Pyrenees is unpredictable at any time of year, the lushness of the surroundings underlining that there's plenty of rain even in summer.

'Plateau de Beille is tougher than Alpe d'Huez.'
Nicolas Portal, Sky team director

his nerve here and in the process half-a-dozen minutes on his rivals. At Ax, the route joins the busy N20 to head down the Ariège valley to Les Cabannes, where the final test begins.

The relief at leaving the N20 behind is quickly tempered by the vicious start of the climb to the Plateau de Beille as it leaves Les Cabannes. The gradient is around ten per cent over the initial five kilometres, the hairpins providing some relief and, consequently, lowering the overall average. It does then ease for a short while, perhaps a kilometre or so, only to return to its previous exacting nature. On the plus side, it is a very peaceful climb. Very little traffic uses this road outside the ski season, as there is not much at the top beyond a café that's mostly used by walkers and cyclists. You're more likely to come across livestock on the road than a car, while the trees on either side of the road add to the serenity of the setting.

After one shortish ramp three-quarters of the way up, the hardest parts of the climb are done. The trees disappear, revealing the top of the mountain and the buzz of the Ariège valley far below. At the Pas de Roland, the road runs onto a saddle that offers views into the Aston valley to the west and to peaks on all sides. Not far beyond is the top of the climb. With just a few buildings next to a large car park, the summit couldn't be

any more different to over-developed Alpe d'Huez and is even a touch underwhelming, but is perhaps all the better for that.

Sportives

The **Ariégeoise** is one of the highlights of the sportive season. First run to Guzet Neige in 1995, the day before Marco Pantani's Tour-stage victory at the Ariège resort, its courses change from year to year, which is one of the attractions for the 5,000-odd riders who take part. Taking place in late June, it always starts in Tarascon-sur-Ariège and tends to finish in either Les Cabannes or Auzat, although in 2016 riders tackling the longest Ariégeoise XXL route faced the challenge of climbing up to Plateau de Beille after crossing the Croix des Morts, Pailhères and Chioula passes for a total of 4,400 metres of vertical gain. There are three shorter options: the standard Ariégeoise, La Montagnole and the relatively benign Passéjade. **Information:** www.cyclosport-ariegeoise.com

Once a regular haunt for the Tour de France, the Montagne Noire features less often on the route of *La Grande Boucle* in the modern era, but remains well worthy of investigation. The ideal way to explore its twisted,

BELOW: Wearing the Tour leader's yellow jersey, Frenchman Thomas Voeckler glides down a Pyrenean descent en route for Plateau de Beille in 2011.

forested roads is in **La Jalabert** sportive, which takes place in late August. Organized by the UV Mazamet cycling club, the event offers two route options. La Laurent, paying tribute to the elder and more celebrated of the two cycling brothers, extends to 115 undulating kilometres. La Nicolas, honouring the younger Jalabert, is 75 kilometres long. Both start in Mazamet and finish on the summit of the Pic de Nore.
Information: www.uvmazamet.fr

The other major sportive that takes place in the Ariège is **La Casartelli**, which commemorates Italy's 1992 Olympic road-race champion Fabio Casartelli, who died when he crashed on the descent of the Col du Portet d'Aspet during the 1995 Tour de France. It takes place over an early September weekend, starting on the Saturday with a time trial from Aspet to the summit of the Portet d'Aspet, passing Casartelli's memorial on the way. There are three sportive routes based on St-Girons on the Sunday: La Casartelli is 132 kilometres in length and features six climbs, including the Portel and Col d'Agnès, which are Tour regulars, while La Découverte is 111 kilometres and La Marco is 47.5 kilometres.
Information: www.cyclosportive-la-casartelli.fr

Other Riding

Long one of the Tour de France's principal battlegrounds, the Aude and Ariège mountains offer a host of famous climbs to tackle, among them Guze Neige near Aulus-les-Bains and Plateau de Bonascre above Ax-les-Thermes. The pretty little town of Chalabre, on the edge of Lac Montbel, or nearby Quillan are good options as a base from which to explore the Aude. There are some stunning rides over the Plateau de Sault from Chalabre towards the Port de Pailhères. These are not so well known, but almost traffic free and for that reason ideal for riders who are less experienced in the mountains and want to build their confidence, particularly on descents. Much busier but still well worth a visit is the magnificent former Cathar stronghold at Montségur. Further west, Foix or Tarascon are good starting points from which to explore the many passes in the Massif de l'Arize that runs towards Oust and St-Girons. You are well advised to avoid the N20 whenever possible by using the minor roads that run along the opposite side of the Ariège valley.

The Birth of a Pyrenean Classic
Luchon–Bayonne, 326km [France]

Route Details
COUNTRY: France
RACE: 1910 Tour de France (stage 10)
ROUTE: Luchon–Bayonne, 326km
TERRAIN: High mountains

Climb Stats
Col de Peyresourde
HEIGHT: 1,569m
ALTITUDE GAINED: 926m
LENGTH: 13.2km
AVERAGE GRADIENT: 7%
MAXIMUM GRADIENT: 11%

Col d'Aspin
HEIGHT: 1,490m
ALTITUDE GAINED: 785m
LENGTH: 12km
AVERAGE GRADIENT: 6.5%
MAXIMUM GRADIENT: 10%

Col du Tourmalet
HEIGHT: 2,115m
ALTITUDE GAINED: 1,268m
LENGTH: 17.2km
AVERAGE GRADIENT: 7.4%
MAXIMUM GRADIENT: 13%

Col du Soulor & Col d'Aubisque
HEIGHT: 1,709m
ALTITUDE GAINED: 1,247m
LENGTH: 30.1km
AVERAGE GRADIENT: 4.1%
MAXIMUM GRADIENT: 12%

Col d'Osquich
HEIGHT: 392m
ALTITUDE GAINED: 251m
LENGTH: 15.2km
AVERAGE GRADIENT: 1.7%
MAXIMUM GRADIENT: 8%

Note: The profile length reflects the suggested route for today's riders to avoid the main roads as suggested on page 200.

OPPOSITE: Looking down from the stadium-like viewpoint at the summit of the Col d'Aspin, as the road climbs up from Arreau.

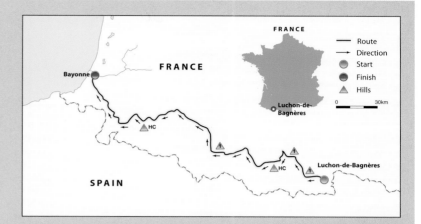

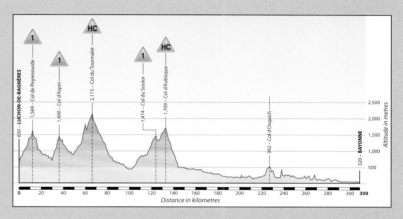

Prior to 1910, the Tour de France covered the length and breadth of the country, but had steered clear of the high mountain passes in the Alps and Pyrenees. It was feared that the race's participants might die of exhaustion if set this challenge, or even end up eaten by wild animals. However, in 1910, after consistently circumventing France's highest country in previous editions, Tour director Henri Desgrange decided that the moment had arrived for the ultimate test of rider and machine.

Believing the loftiest alpine passes were no place to experiment, Desgrange settled on two stages in the Pyrenees for this fearsome innovation. The first, from Perpignan to Luchon, crossed four passes – the Port, Portet, Portet d'Aspet and Ares. Desgrange saw enough that day to absent himself from the following stage, leaving his assistant, Victor Breyer, in charge.

It was a canny move on Desgrange's part, given the stick Breyer and his organizing team received from the riders. Stage winner and eventual champion Octave Lapize, who took 14 hours to complete the 326-kilometre stage, denounced them as 'assassins' as he crossed the summit of the Col d'Aubisque. He threatened to abandon but rode on, confirming in the wake of his victory that, 'Desgrange is indeed an assassin'.

The riders' ordeal began in Luchon-de-Bagnères at half-past three in the morning, thanks to the organizers' desire for a late-afternoon finish

in Bayonne. Anyone brave enough to attempt to emulate them ought to start at a similar hour, although for most this stage is better tackled over two days, with an overnight stop either before or after the Aubisque.

The climbing begins right from the off. Rising straight out of Luchon, the Peyresourde is a wonderful ascent, bordered by lush mountain pasture given a flush of rich colour by wildflowers. The road is wide, well surfaced and, although quite challenging, is not as tough as much of the climbing that lies ahead. Riding up through its sweeping curves, it is worth remembering that Lapize reached its summit in 57 minutes in 1910, riding in the dark on a heavy, single-speed bike on what was then an unsealed road.

The descent on the Peyresourde's western flank into the Aure valley is fast thanks to the good condition of the road, but not frighteningly so. Within minutes, you're into Arreau and, after a few twists and turns, onto the lower slopes of the Col d'Aspin. Neither as high nor as long as the Peyresourde, the Aspin has a similar profile to its neighbour and is just as attractive. It starts gently, winding up through woodland and soon delivering impressive views over Arreau and the valley below, as well as towards the saddle high above where the crest of the climb lies.

As the road moves away from the Aure valley and advances on the pass, it opens out onto a steep mountainside. The gradient gets a little tougher at this point, but the views south towards Saint-Lary Soulan and

the peaks on the Spanish border take a little of the edge off the increased effort. That effort needs to be maintained almost all the way to the summit, but those views continue to act as an analgesic for the legs and the lungs.

Leaving the open top, the road cuts down through forest and glades where cattle graze. There are often lots of them at the tiny ski station of Payolle about halfway down the descent, so caution is advised. Below here, the gradient is quite shallow, to the extent that you might even have to resort to pedalling occasionally to maintain momentum down to the Adour valley.

The road reaches Sainte-Marie-de-Campan, where the 17-kilometre climb of the Col du Tourmalet, the highest road pass in the French Pyrenees, begins. This is an ideal moment to pause, particularly as the

village is home to one of the Tour's most iconic locations. In the 1913 Tour, Frenchman Eugène Christophe, who was lying second overall and was leading the stage, realized that his front forks had broken as he was descending the Tourmalet. The rules prohibited Christophe from taking a replacement bike, so he had to lug his ten kilometres down the mountain to the forge in Sainte-Marie-de-Campan to fashion a repair. Unable to receive any assistance and delayed for four hours by the incident, he received a further three-minute time penalty because the blacksmith's young assistant had worked the bellows for him. The forge is now marked with a plaque.

Riding away from Sainte-Marie-de-Campan, the gradient is quite benign for the opening third of the climb, the road passing through verdant

ABOVE: Having crested the 2,100-metre Col du Tourmalet, the Tour's riders begin the long descent to Luz-St-Sauveur at the foot of the pass.

pasture. The task gets much more serious above the hamlet of Gripp, though, the incline steepening and rising quickly away from the edge of the stream that the road had previously been following. Cutting directly through thick and often mist-shrouded woodland that conceals any hint of what lies ahead, the climb is stubbornly steep and demanding until the first glimpse of the 1960s concrete tower blocks of La Mongie confirms that the worst is almost over.

Unimaginative and in fact just plain ugly, La Mongie tosses up the steepest ramp on this side of the mountain. Once conquered, though, the gradient does ease for the final three kilometres to the crest of the pass, where a statue commemorates Octave Lapize's feat of being the first rider to this summit.

In contrast to the east flank of the pass, which runs through a precipitous V-shaped valley, the western side is open and expansive, the course of the road clearly visible as it switchbacks down past the resort of Superbarèges, which is far less conspicuous than La Mongie, to Barèges itself. Dropping through the hairpins below this pretty village to Luz-St-Sauveur, the route turns north towards Lourdes, running through the Gorges du Luz to reach Argelès-Gazost and the start of the climb of the Aubisque.

The Tour's second-most-visited climb after the Tourmalet, the Aubisque is not as high or as tough, especially from this side, which climbs initially to the Col du Soulor. The approach to the Soulor begins in cadence-sapping fashion and ends in the same way, but once past that initial ramp, this is a climb to savour as it rises in shallow steps through pastureland, with snowy peaks filling the view ahead. Running straight to start with, above Aucun it twists and turns through woods and meadows before rising quite steeply for three kilometres to reach the landing at the top of the pass.

After descending for a short while, the road begins to climb towards the Aubisque on one of the most sensational bits of road anywhere in the Pyrenees. Cut into the cliff face ascending almost vertically towards the Pic de la Latte de Bazen, the narrow ledge offers an immense panorama, although the long drop just off to the right may grab most riders' attention more. The nervy feel may increase a little further on, as the road exits a tunnel through the rock to reach an even more precarious perch and passes a plaque marking the point where Wim Van Est, the first Dutch rider to wear the Tour's yellow jersey in 1951, plunged over the edge in that race. Van Est fell 70 metres, but survived, teammates and fans hauling him back up with inner tubes that had been tied together.

Beyond this balcony, the Aubisque's summit is only three kilometres of easy climbing away. Dropping quickly through the resort of Gourette and the once plush but now fading spa of Eaux-Bonnes, the road runs due north down the Ossau valley, passing the turn onto another Tour favourite, the Col de Marie-Blanque, to reach Arudy, where it forks through the beautiful Bager forest. This sets the tone for the next 60 kilometres of riding, the mountains now all but forgotten as the route follows picturesque country roads along meandering river valleys, passing through Arette, Tardets and Mauléon-Licharre, one of the main centres in the French Basque Country.

This small town is also the start of the final significant climb over the Col d'Osquich, from which there are fantastic views over the snowy ridge of the Pyrenees. After dipping down into Saint-Jean-Pied-de-Port, the 1910 route turned northwest to Biarritz and Bayonne, following the River Nive almost to the sea. This is now one of the main routes across this border region, so an alternative may be preferable, perhaps via the minor roads that reach Hasparren and continue on to Bayonne. It was here, in 1910, that Octave Lapize had to sprint to beat Italy's Pierino Albini after 14 hours of racing a stage that would change the face of road racing.

ABOVE LEFT: There's a wonderful view from close to the top of the Col d'Aspin, across the peaks in the central Pyrenean region, the summits rippling away into the distance.
ABOVE RIGHT: Riders flick through the bends heading down the Tourmalet.
OPPOSITE: A huge crowd awaits the riders at the top of the Col d'Aspin.

'It wasn't anything superhuman because we weren't supermen. I'm the proof, a man like anybody else.'

Gustave Garrigou, the only man to ride every metre of this 1910 stage

Sportives

Named in tribute to cycling brothers Roger and Guy Lapébie and their racing sons, Christian and Serge, **La Lapébie** is part of the Grand Trophée series. Starting and finishing in Luchon, it takes place in early September and features three routes: the 157-kilometre Masters crosses the Ares, Larrieu, Menté and Port de Balès passes; the 124-kilometre Senior misses the Larrieu but includes the other three passes; and the 69-kilometre rando loops around over the Port de Balès, which was only opened in 2006 but has quickly become a Tour favourite. **Information:** www.grandtrophee.fr

The organizers of the hugely popular Marmotte sportive that takes place in the Alps have established a sister event with a similar profile in the Pyrenees. Taking place in August and extending to 174 kilometres, the **Marmotte Granfondo Pyrénées** starts in Argelès-Gazost and finishes at the summit of Luz Ardiden, having crossed the Tourmalet and Soulor to amass 5,000 metres of vertical gain. **Information:** www.sport.be/marmottegranfondoseries/fr

Spain's biggest sportive is the 200-kilometre **Quebrantahuesos**, the bone-breaker, which starts on the Spanish side of the border in Sabiñánigo, crosses the Col du Somport to enter France, where it continues over the Marie-Blanque and returns to Spain via the Col du Pourtalet. The event gets its name from the vultures that can be found in this region of the Pyrenees, notably on the cliffs that dominate the Ossau valley near Laruns. The birds drop animal carcasses onto rocks in order to get at the bone marrow, earning them their rather gruesome name. The sister event to the 9,000-rider Quebrantahuesos is the Treparriscos, which covers 85 kilometres on the Spanish side of the border. **Information:** www.quebrantahuesos.com

Early July's **La Pyrénéenne** offers three routes starting in Bagnères-de-Bigorre, one of the principal cycling centres in these mountains, and finishing at Lac de Payolle, halfway down the Col d'Aspin. The Quatre

Vallées route, the longest at 180 kilometres, crosses the Tourmalet via Barèges, the stunning Hourquette d'Ancizan and the Col d'Aspin. The 125-kilometre Deux Vallées features the Tourmalet, while the runs out from Bagnères to the Lac de Payolle and back again make for a 40-kilometre total. **Information:** www.lapyreneenne.a3w.fr

Other Riding

As with the Mediterranean end of the range, the best way to explore the central and Basque areas of the Pyrenees is to decide on a base and venture out from there. There is no one best place, but Bagnères-de-Bigorre and Bagnères-de-Luchon (usually known as Luchon) are close to a large number and variety of climbs and also offer plenty of options with regard to dining and accommodation. Argelès-Gazost is another good option. It is smaller, but very well placed for the Aubisque and Tourmalet passes, as well as Hautacam, Luz Ardiden and Cauterets.

BELOW: Looking down from the top of the Tourmalet towards Barèges and the road that eventually leads onto the Soulor and Aubisque passes.

The Climb That Downed Wiggo
Avilés–Alto de l'Angliru, 142km [Spain]

When Sir Bradley Wiggins was at his road-racing peak, he achieved every target that he set himself with one exception. After crashing out of the 2011 Tour de France with a broken collar bone but still wanting to confirm his new-found status as a contender for the major three-week tours, the Briton turned his attention to the Vuelta a España. Going into the final week of the race, Wiggins looked well set to claim the title. At the end of a very mountainous stage 14, the Londoner's closest challenger was his Sky teammate, Chris Froome, who had surprised everyone with his performances. Dutchman Bauke Mollema was more than half a minute back in third, while Spain's Juan José Cobo was almost a minute down in fourth. A Sky victory looked odds on. But Wiggins had one immense hurdle to clear in the form of a climb that many rate as the toughest in professional cycling.

The toughest ascents are often described as resembling animal tracks that have had tarmac thrown down on them to make them passable. In the heart of the Sierra del Aramo, little more than a dozen kilometres

BELOW: Sitting between the parched plains of northern Spain and the cool waters of the Bay of Biscay, the mountains of Asturias are often shrouded in mist, although it doesn't tend to persist for long.

south of the city of Oviedo, there is a climb that exactly fits that description. Rising through verdant pastureland, the Alto de l'Angliru, also known as El Gamonal, is a climb to nowhere unless you're one of the local cattle farmers.

First introduced to the Vuelta in 1999, when flamboyant Spanish climber José María Jiménez, the brother-in-law of the 2008 Tour de France champion Carlos Sastre, was victorious, the Angliru is one of a handful of ascents guaranteed to extract the spring from the heels of even the most accomplished of mountain goats. Commencing in the village of La Vega, the Angliru has two halves. The first is tough and, after a short section in a saddle between two ridges, the second is simply ridiculous. Averaging a touch more than ten per cent over 12.5 kilometres, the final half-dozen kilometres before the short drop to the line average four points above that, enough to ensure that all the action there takes place in slow motion.

Coming onto this section in 2011 wearing the gold leader's jersey, Wiggins didn't respond to an attack from Cobo, choosing to use Froome as his shepherd. However, approaching the steepling Cueña les Cabres section, where the gradient almost touches 25 per cent, Wiggins, his face twisted with agony, slid gradually away from Froome's wheel. For the next minute or so, Sky were in limbo. Stick or twist? By the time Froome had been given free rein, Cobo, nicknamed 'The Buffalo' for his brute strength, had the stage won and the gold jersey was his. Froome chipped away at his lead for the next week, but the Spaniard held on to win by 13 seconds, the Angliru making all the difference to his success.

The greatest racing day of Cobo's career began in the port of Avilés, to the north of Oviedo. This is the heartland of Spain's dairy industry, and after a few kilometres it's very apparent why, as the route rolls constantly through pasture that's kept lush and verdant by the weather fronts that roll in off the Atlantic. The terrain is what the Spanish describe as *rompepiernas*, or leg-breaking. There's one little climb after another until the route drops into the Narcea valley for the easiest riding all day.

Heading east from Cornellana, it begins to climb again, passing through countryside that has a touch of rainforest about it, thanks to an abundance of greenery and the mist that often shrouds the hillsides. At Udrión, the route begins to track south alongside the River Trubia and loftier peaks begin to loom. The valley narrows until river and road are running tightly together, separated only by the Senda del Oso ('Bear's Path') hiking and biking trail that runs for 25 kilometres through this region, which is home to a brown bear conservation area.

RIGHT: It's rare to see Bradley Wiggins looking as pained as this on a bike, especially when he was at his peak as a stage racer. His expression says everything about how difficult the Angliru is.

'At several points on the climb I felt as though time had stopped. You keep spinning the pedals and, on those occasions when you raise your head, you realize that you've barely advanced.'

Pedro Delgado, Tour de France and two-time Vuelta winner

Soon after the valley opens out again, the route reaches Villanueva and turns left towards Tenebredo, this change of tack also signalling a change of emphasis. Half of the ride is done but all of the serious climbing still lies ahead, and it begins immediately. Cutting across the front of the Bar Las Xanas, the road rears up to almost 15 per cent before settling back to nearer nine for a couple of kilometres. Passing the hamlet of Tenebredo, the gradient increases once more and this time there's no let-up as it stays wickedly steep for a lung-straining kilometre.

The fast descent that follows offers glimpses of Oviedo through the hills ahead, but the city quickly disappears behind the hills on its southern flanks as the route tracks east along the Nalón river valley. Here, the sight of the La Viesca coal mine offers an abrupt reminder that, as well as being a dairy-producing centre, Asturias has long been one of Spain's industrial engines.

From Soto de Ribera, the route swaps the Nalón for the Caudal, travelling due south on a main road with a very wide and bike-friendly shoulder. A right turn towards Las Mazas onto the AS231 offers the opportunity to head directly to the foot of the Angliru, missing out the urban sections before and after Mieres, but taking this option does mean missing the traditional stepping stone to the final climb, the Alto del Cordal, which has also provoked a good deal of debate in the past.

In truth, the road through Mieres and beyond isn't that bad because the nearby motorway takes most of the traffic. It improves a good deal when it crosses the river at Figaredo, and much more when it turns under the motorway and railway viaducts towards Riosa for an encounter with the controversial Cordal. In 2002, heavy rain turned the very tricky descent off this pass into a scary lottery that resulted in many riders sliding off. David Millar was among those who went down, although the Scot did manage to get back in the saddle and ride up the Angliru, only to lay down his bike a metre short of the line and quit the race in protest at the conditions the riders had endured on the Cordal.

Like the Tenebredo it begins sharply, soon leaving the hum of the motorway behind, then eases off as it climbs through woodland. There's just an occasional rhythm-disrupting ramp until Soterraña, where the real difficulties begin. There are several ramps of between 14 and 16 per cent, the roughness of the surface adding to the complications. After 1,500 metres of pain, relief comes thanks to stunning views in all directions from the summit. The road surface doesn't improve on the descent off the Cordal, which faces north and is very prone to dampness, especially under the trees. The saving grace is that it's not as steep as the southern flank.

The road drops into La Vega and straight onto the Angliru. For the opening half-dozen kilometres, you're left wondering what all the fuss is about. There are some hard sections, but nothing extraordinary as the road snakes upwards past farms and hamlets. It even plateaus at a picnic and recreation area, the long and wide saddle offering extensive views to the north and south. Make the most of them, as you're likely to spend the next half hour staring at your handlebars.

Boards at the roadside detailing the history of the climb announce the start of something much more serious, one of them describing 'The Hell of the Vuelta'. Graffiti on the road backs that up, announcing, 'Welcome to hell'. That begins with the 22-per-cent Les Cabanes ramp, soon after the road has started climbing seriously again. There are similar ramps every kilometre or so from this point on. The next, Lagos, at a mere 14.5, is the only one of them below the 20-per-cent mark. Most days, they carry you closer to the low cloud that regularly envelops these green peaks.

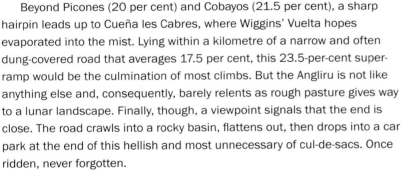

Beyond Picones (20 per cent) and Cobayos (21.5 per cent), a sharp hairpin leads up to Cueña les Cabres, where Wiggins' Vuelta hopes evaporated into the mist. Lying within a kilometre of a narrow and often dung-covered road that averages 17.5 per cent, this 23.5-per-cent super-ramp would be the culmination of most climbs. But the Angliru is not like anything else and, consequently, barely relents as rough pasture gives way to a lunar landscape. Finally, though, a viewpoint signals that the end is close. The road crawls into a rocky basin, flattens out, then drops into a car park at the end of this hellish and most unnecessary of cul-de-sacs. Once ridden, never forgotten.

Sportives

The Angliru may steal most of the attention, but arguably the most illustrious summit finish in Asturias is at the Lagos de Covadonga, which have featured on the Vuelta route on 19 occasions since their introduction in 1983 and have been compared to Alpe d'Huez. The 16-kilometre climb is the centrepiece of early June's **Clásica Lagos de Covadonga**. The event, which extends to 110 kilometres, starts in Cangas de Onis and crosses two smaller climbs before the final ascent, where the steepest section is known as La Huesera, 'the boneyard'.
Information: www.cctnavastur.es

Surprisingly, there is not a well-established sportive that features the Angliru. However, a mountain time-trial does take place on the mountain in early October. Starting in Riosa, the **Angliru Cronoescalada** also features a walking race up the mountain.
Information: www.carreraangliru.blogspot.co.uk

Other Riding

Despite the Vuelta's recent preference for the mountains of Spain's northern provinces as the race's key battleground, Asturias, Cantabria and Galicia don't receive anything like the same numbers of foreign cyclists as the regions along the country's Mediterranean coast and, of course, Majorca, long a mecca for riders from across Europe. There are several reasons behind this, particularly comparatively poor communications and an unpredictable climate that resembles that of northern Europe more than the south. However, all three provinces have much to recommend them.

Long a cycling backwater, Galicia has embraced the sport much more since the millennium. Thanks partly to the exploits of local star Oscar Pereiro, who won the Tour de France in 2006, and more extensively to the enthusiasm of the regional government, which backed a pro team for several seasons and now plays host to the Vuelta most years, cycling has been embraced very warmly. It is a very rugged region and there are climbs aplenty, but the coastline is arguably Galicia's most outstanding feature. To the east, on the border between Galicia and León, the Ancares National Park is another natural wonder where the standout test is the Ancares pass.

ABOVE LEFT: Mist often lingers around these Asturian peaks, which collect the weather that comes off the ocean
ABOVE RIGHT: Once away from the towns and cities nearer the coast, the roads tend to be very quiet indeed.
OPPOSITE LEFT: The smaller mountain roads in this area tend to make little allowance for the gradient, often taking the straightest line rather than switching back and forth.
OPPOSITE RIGHT: The route dips and rises through pine stands early on.

Often compared to the Mortirolo, it is a tad easier than the Italian climb but wins out handsomely over it in terms of looks, as it's generally regarded as one of the most beautiful in Spain.

The Asturian coast is also dramatic, huge headlands dropping into tight coves where the Atlantic surf thumps in. The real treats are inland, though. Almost every year the Vuelta organizers unearth a gem of a climb. The Farrapona, Ermita de Alba and the Camperona are the most recent to have joined local classics such as the Cotobello, Cobertoria and the Naranco, which sits right above Oviedo and is the region's iconic ascent thanks to its connections with the great Asturian climber of the 1970s, José Manuel Fuente, known as 'El Tarangu'.

Further to the east, Cantabria, the home region of three-time world champion Oscar Freire and Juan José Cobo, is another almost traffic-free haven for cyclists. The very taxing Peña Cabarga, set above the dramatic bay at Santander, has particular relevance for Cobo as it was there that he managed to withstand Chris Froome's final attempt to unseat him as he headed for victory in the 2011 Vuelta. Deeper into the province, the mountains west of Reinosa are also impressive, the Alto Campoo only the most renowned of them.

RIGHT: The weather can be unpredictable, changing quickly in these mountains, with mist rolling across the peaks.

Fact File The Climb That Downed Wiggo

Route Details

COUNTRY: Spain
RACE: 2011 Vuelta a España (stage 15)
ROUTE: Avilés–Alto de l'Angliru, 142km
TERRAIN: Mountain valleys and high-altitude finish

Climb Stats

Alto de Tenebredo
HEIGHT: 510m
ALTITUDE GAINED: 326m
LENGTH: 3.2km
AVERAGE GRADIENT: 10.3%
MAXIMUM GRADIENT: 15%

Alto del Cordal
HEIGHT: 797m
ALTITUDE GAINED: 505m
LENGTH: 5.5km
AVERAGE GRADIENT: 9.2%
MAXIMUM GRADIENT: 16%

Alto de l'Angliru
HEIGHT: 1,570m
ALTITUDE GAINED: 1,265m
LENGTH: 12.6km
AVERAGE GRADIENT: 10%
MAXIMUM GRADIENT: 24%

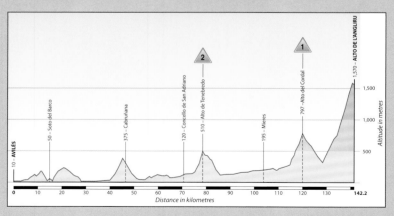

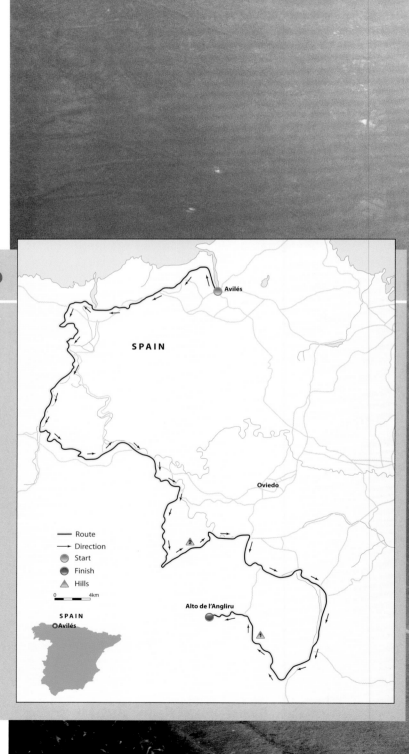

A Bird's-Eye View of Madrid
Segovia–Bola del Mundo, 170.7km [Spain]

BELOW: Cutting through thick pine forest, the roads in the Sierra de Guadarrama are wonderfully quiet.

The major stage races all conclude with a big-city finale that provides some high-octane thrills on the television, but which take place on courses that are hardly conducive to amateurs searching for some kicks of their own. Riding laps of the Tour de France's traditional Champs-Élysées circuit in Paris wouldn't be much fun at all on any normal day, when it would be choked with traffic, and the same goes for the Giro d'Italia and Vuelta a España finishes in Milan and Madrid, respectively. This stage offers a solution, though. While it doesn't venture into Madrid, it is possible to see the centre of the Spanish capital from a number of points on the route, including the dramatic high-rise finale.

The location for it is the southern end of the Sierra de Guadarrama massif to the north of Madrid. This is the regular training terrain for multiple Grand Tour winner Alberto Contador, who lives in Pinto to the south of the city, and a host of other pros. For bike-mad Madrileños, this is their favourite cycling playground. There are many climbs, most of them little used by motorized traffic.

The route begins next to the La Faisanera golf club on the outskirts of Segovia, although the beautiful World Heritage city is undoubtedly a more appealing starting point. The advantage of opting for La Faisanera is that it lies on the descent back down from the finish, making it the ideal choice for those planning a circular ride. There's also a bike path running parallel to the road, which makes for a hassle-free warm-up as you head away from the peaks where this ride will finish. The path swings right to follow the Segovia ring road for a few hundred metres, before zig-zagging on the back roads through Palazuelos de Eresma and San Cristóbal de Segovia to meet the N110 at Torrecaballeros.

Turning northeast to run parallel to the Guadarrama mountains, the road runs through countryside befitting a spaghetti western, which did use locations in Spain, although far to the south in the Tabernas desert near Almería. There's barely a kink in what is essentially a flat road for the next 20 kilometres, which makes for hard going if the wind is coming from the north or east on this central plateau that sits more than 1,000 metres above sea level.

If that wind is blowing, relief comes with a right turn towards Navafría. Continuing through the little town, the route begins to climb, initially through scattered stands of pine, before entering thick forest on the ten-kilometre stretch of the quiet and rather wonderful Puerto de Navafría. There are no significant changes to the gradient, which sticks at between five and seven per cent for the most part. It's the perfect way to warm up your legs before the harder tests to come.

The summit sits on the border between the provinces of Segovia and Madrid, the road dropping just as steadily and picturesquely to Buitrago del Lozoya, from where it skirts around the northern shore of the Pinilla reservoir. A straight of several kilometres and then a second after a sharp right turn leads to Canencia, and then on to pass of the same name. A

ABOVE: Climbing the cement road to the Bola del Mundo high above the Navacerrada pass.
OPPOSITE: These climbs are densely forested for the most part.

little shorter than the Navafría, but with the same very attractive aspect, the Canencia has some steeper ramps near its summit, from where the road dips gently down to Miraflores and immediately onto the start of the Morcuera pass, a Vuelta favourite.

The most taxing climb so far, the Morcuera begins with long, tree-lined straights where the gradient hardly varies. However, reaching a ruined hut three kilometres below the summit, its ramps become more severe, although not to the point where it should ruffle competent climbers too much. The large plateau at the top makes for a good lunch stop before the descent down on the longer, but less severe, northern side of the pass to Rascafría.

The pattern of climb, descent, climb continues with a left turn into Rascafría to begin the Puerto de Cotos. Arrowing initially through pine woods that throw much-needed shade across the road in the summer

months, it offers no serious difficulty beyond its length. At 14 kilometres it is the longest pass of the day so far, and that accumulation of uphill effort is sure to be taking a toll on even the best climbers. The straights give way to more meandering progress on the higher sections of the pass, until the last run up to the broad summit, from which there is access to the Valdesquí resort.

A rolling seven-kilometre section along this ridge breaks the established up-and-down pattern. As the road twists, there are occasional views up to the red-and-white telecommunications masts on the mountain above. That is the Bola del Mundo, but that comes later. First up is one of Spain's most renowned passes, the Alto de Navacerrada, which is first reached at the end of that seven-kilometre stretch and will, later, provide the launchpad for the lung-busting finale, although the option is there to take it on immediately

and miss the long loop down to Guadarrama and back.

The drop off the Navacerrada is not overly steep, but its straightness makes it very fast. This road can be busy and is quite open to the wind, so take care. After eight kilometres, a fork to the right leads to Cercedilla and then onto the final plummet into Guadarrama, where a quick switch through the streets leads onto the M614. This runs parallel to and a kilometre or so east of the road down from Cercedilla, so you'll have a good idea of what's now in store.

Gaining 300 metres in altitude over ten kilometres, the route returns to the main road up the Navacerrada pass, where the gradient becomes markedly steeper. Much more open than the earlier passes, the road provides rapid access to the ski fields at and beyond the top of the pass, taking the shortest line wherever possible. If there's a headwind, it can become quite a sapping grind up to the resort hotels and the huge expanse of car park at the summit.

Just over the top of the pass, the road that provides access to the telecommunications equipment at the Bola del Mundo jags back at almost 180 degrees. Beyond a barrier that checks car drivers but is easily negotiated by cyclists, it leaps sharply up, quickly leaving the resort behind. Made of concrete with a rough, rippled surface, the track is broken in parts, but passable. The road's surface may be an irritant, but it's the angle that's the principal difficulty. There are several sections close to 20 per cent, with the steepest right at the end. By that point, though, the masts are encouragingly close, and once you've hauled yourself up to them, this crowning achievement is rewarded with magnificent views in every direction.

BELOW: The Vuelta's riders have got their focus on reaching the Bola del Mundo rather than the spectacular view it offers towards Madrid.

Fact File A Bird's-Eye View of Madrid

Route Details

Country: Spain
Race: 2012 Vuelta a España (stage 20)
Route: Segovia–Bola del Mundo, 170.7km
Terrain: Mountainous

Climb Stats

Puerto de Navafría
HEIGHT: 1,773m
ALTITUDE GAINED: 565m
LENGTH: 10.9 km
AVERAGE GRADIENT: 5.2%
MAXIMUM GRADIENT: 7%

Puerto de Canencia
HEIGHT: 1,515m
ALTITUDE GAINED: 390m
LENGTH: 8km
AVERAGE GRADIENT: 4.9%
MAXIMUM GRADIENT: 10%

Puerto de la Morcuera
HEIGHT: 1,796m
ALTITUDE GAINED: 623m
LENGTH: 9.2km
AVERAGE GRADIENT: 6.8%
MAXIMUM GRADIENT: 12%

Puerto de Navacerrada and Bola del Mundo
HEIGHT: 2,247m
ALTITUDE GAINED: 987m
LENGTH: 11.4km
AVERAGE GRADIENT: 8.7%
MAXIMUM GRADIENT: 20%

Puerto de Cotos
HEIGHT: 1,830m
ALTITUDE GAINED: 637m
LENGTH: 14km
AVERAGE GRADIENT: 4.6%
MAXIMUM GRADIENT: 8%

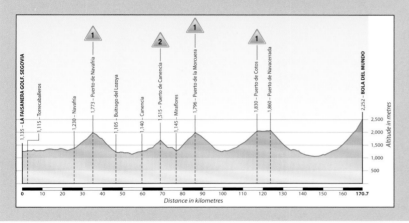

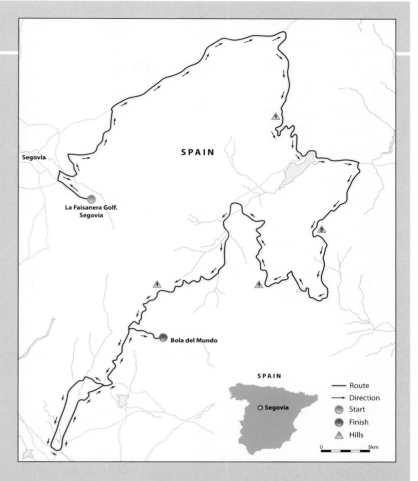

OPPOSITE: Russian Vladimir Karpets is urged on by fans as he approaches the steepest section of the climb to the Bola del Mundo.

Sportives

Starting and finishing in Colmenar Viejo, early June's **Desafío Puertos del Guadarrama** extends to 158 kilometres and covers much of the same ground as the 2010 Vuelta stage, notably the Morcuera and Canencia passes. The former features a timed section between Miraflores and the summit. In 2015, veteran Spanish pro Francisco Mancebo set a new record for this 9.2-kilometre section, covering it in an astonishing 23 minutes and 13 seconds. **Information:** www.fmciclismo.com/fmc

Over on the southern side of Madrid in Colmenar de Oreja, the **Madrid Extrema** offers a variety of challenges over a mid-April weekend. The event combines road and mountain biking in the shape of the two-day Heroica, which kicks off with an 85-kilometre MTB race on the Saturday and concludes with the 170-kilometre Gran Fondo on the Sunday. If you don't fancy the mountain biking, the MX Road events on the Sunday comprise the Gran Fondo, with 2,250 metres of vertical gain. If that looks too much, there is a 100-kilometre Medio Fondo with half as much climbing. **Information:** www.madridxtrema.com

Held as a tribute to Segovia's greatest cyclist, who was the winner of the 1988 Tour de France as well as two editions of the Vuelta, mid-August's **Marcha Pedro Delgado** covers several passes in the Sierra de Guadarrama. With Segovia as its start/finish, the 164-kilometre course heads up the northern side of the Navacerrada and continues over the Morcuera, Canencia and Navafría passes. **Information:** www.pedrodelgado.com

Other Riding

Lying immediately to the west of Madrid is another of the Vuelta's regular haunts, the wild and largely empty Sierra de Gredos. A regular training location for 2008 Tour winner Carlos Sastre, who hails from the little town of El Barraco, the Gredos massif features some celebrated climbs, including the Serranillos, Peña Negra and Navalmoral passes and a beautiful stretch of road running east to west between San Martín del Pimpollar and El Barco de Ávila. The smaller roads to the east of Madrid towards the lovely town of Cuenca are also well worth exploring. In keeping with Spain's status as Europe's most mountainous country after Austria, they also feature plenty of climbing.

Index

Picture Credits

© Gruber Images
1, 2, 6, 8, 11, 13, 14, 16, 18, 20, 24, 25, 26, 29, 30, 32, 35, 36, 37, 38, 40, 42, 45, 46, 50, 53, 54, 56, 58, 60, 62, 63, 64, 67, 68, 70, 72, 73, 74, 85, 89, 106, 108, 111, 113, 114, 122, 124, 126, 127, 128 (both), 129, 130, 132, 133, 134, 136, 137, 138, 140, 141, 142, 143, 144, 146, 148 (both), 151, 152, 154, 155, 156, 157, 158, 160, 161, 162, 163, 164, 166, 167, 168, 170, 188, 192, 196, 198, 200 (both), 201, 202, 204, 208 (both), 209 (both), 211, 222, endpapers

Shutterstock
5

Getty Images
10, 22, 49, 104, 172, 175, 177, 179,

Corbis
77, 78, 79, 80, 82, 86 (inset), 91, 92, 93, 94, 96, 98, 101, 102, 116, 117, 118, 121, 180, 182, 184, 187, 190, 191, 194, 207, 212, 214, 215, 216, 218,

©Tim De Waele/www.tdwsport.com
86 (main image), 174 (both)

Press Association Images
100

Acknowledgements

I would like to thank Richard Green and Lucy Warburton at Aurum Publishing for supporting the idea for *Ultimate Étapes* from the off, and also my editor at Aurum, Melissa Smith, whose insights and enthusiasm were invaluable. My gratitude also goes to Iain MacGregor, my riding partner at the Tour of Flanders sportive, which provided the inspiration for this book.

As always, I offer my thanks to my literary agent, David Luxton, and his team at David Luxton Associates. Finally, I would like to offer my thanks and love to my wife, Elaine, and to my children, Lewis and Eleanor, who are discovering the delights of the mid-ride café stop and learning that going uphill can sometimes be almost as much fun as going down. I dedicate this book to all three of you.

Quarto is the authority on a wide range of topics.
Quarto educates, entertains and enriches the lives of
our readers — enthusiasts and lovers of hands-on living.

www.QuartoKnows.com

First published in Great Britain
2016 by Aurum Press Ltd
74—77 White Lion Street
Islington
London N1 9PF

A catalogue record for this book is available from the British Library.

ISBN 978 1 78131 590 3

10 9 8 7 6 5 4 3 2 1
2020 2019 2018 2017 2016

Designed by The Urban Ant Ltd.
Printed in China